Environmental Anthropology

Third Edition

Environmental Anthropology

From Pigs to Policies

Third Edition

Patricia K. Townsend

State University of New York, Buffalo

WAVELAND

PRESS, INC.

Long Grove, Illinois

For information about this book, contact:
Waveland Press, Inc.
4180 IL Route 83, Suite 101
Long Grove, IL 60047-9580
(847) 634-0081
info@waveland.com
www.waveland.com

Photo Credits
Cover–Thailand drought. Photo by Chaiwat Srijankul (Shutterstock).
Frontispiece–Cowherds in Koupela, Burkina Faso. Photo by Gilles Paire
(Shutterstock). *Chapter 1*–The author in Yapatawi village, Papua New
Guinea, 1967. Photo by William H. Townsend. *Chapter 2*–Paiute Indians
in Cedar, Utah, 1872. Photo by Timothy H. O'Sullivan (Wikimedia Commons). *Chapter 3*–Culina (Peru) man making a fish net. Photo by William
H. Townsend. *Chapter 4*–Saniyo dancer wearing pig's tusk armlets and casso-
wary plumes, 1967. Photo by William H. Townsend. *Chapter 5*–Culina (Peru)
hunter and peccary. Photo by William H. Townsend. *Chapter 6*–Machu Picchu.
Photo by Thomas J. Curtin. *Chapter 7*–A haul truck being loaded with dirt
and ore at an Australian iron mine. Photo by Gingerss (Shutterstock). *Chapter
8*–Nuclear explosion. Photo by CUTWORLD (Shutterstock). *Chapter 9*–Inuit
fisherman. Photo by Ann McElroy. *Chapter 10*–Informal settlements in Cape
Town, South Africa. Photo by Moobatto (Shutterstock). *Chapter 11*–Sago palm
forest in Papua New Guinea. Photo by William H. Townsend. *Chapter 13*–Taos
Pueblo cemetery and ruins. *Chapter 14*–Junk cars crushed and ready for recycling. Photo by LYSVIK PHOTOS (Shutterstock).

Contents

Contents

Preface

My interest in the subject matter of this book goes back to studying grade school geography at one of the last one-room schools in rural southwestern Michigan and daydreaming by the creek in our back pasture about going to the faraway places I had studied. More directly, it dates from an excellent undergraduate education at the University of Michigan where the influence of Marshall Sahlins and Kenneth Pike converged in a few short semesters to set my intellectual course, even though both of my first anthropology teachers soon moved off in quite different directions from the one I have taken. The first six chapters of the book reflect that personal and disciplinary history, while the final chapters reflect my conviction that, of the various scholarly disciplines, anthropology has both an appropriate degree of humility and a broad enough vision to address the environmental mess that we humans have made.

The second and third editions have been revised throughout to include new research. A new chapter (8) deals with the environmental impact of war, writing as I am in the midst of the destruction of Syria and, in Iraq and Afghanistan, the longest war in which the United States has yet engaged. For this third edition, I especially thank my husband Bill, who has encouraged and reassured me by more than fifty years of unwavering belief in the importance of my calling. As in earlier editions, the enthusiasm of Tom Curtin and Jeni Ogilvie at Waveland has kept me at the computer, as have helpful words from Ann McElroy.

Chapter One

Introduction

W hen I went to live with the Saniyo-Hiyowe of **Papua New Guinea** in 1966 as a 24-year-old graduate student in anthropology, in many ways I had to begin as a baby. There were no dictionaries or grammars of their language. I could not study it in advance but only by bumbling along, pointing to a house or a pig and imitating the response, *"wesi"* or *"fei."* I had to hope that what I was learning was really the word "house" or "pig" and not "finger" or "what the heck does she want?"

The villagers welcomed my husband, Bill, and me warmly and tried to teach me manners. It is rude to point with your finger; instead you gesture with your lower lip. You are not supposed to watch someone eat. You can pet the pigs, but you must kick the dogs, to discourage them from hanging around trying to grab food. Because I thought I was a reasonably good hiker, it was most humiliating to have mere children or old ladies try to give me a hand as I felt my way across bridges consisting of a single skinny log across deep mud holes. All of this to learn before I could even begin to record their knowledge of the tropical forest environment.

Eventually, in nearly two years of fieldwork, Bill and I collected 178 plants for the Papua and New Guinea herbarium and created a glossary of plant and animal terms as part of my dictionary of the language and description of the **culture**. Bill, who is a civil engineer, mapped the immediate area and documented the use of stone tools to cut trees, discovering that it takes a man skilled in using both a stone tool and a steel axe about four times longer to cut a tree with the stone tool (W. Townsend 1969).

The most important part of the biotic environment for my study was the sago palm, *Metroxylon sagu,* because it was the carbohydrate staple of the diet (Townsend 1974). Sago starch was a monotonous 85 percent of the food eaten. Many other foods were eaten in small amounts as merely a garnish or snack. These included fish, meat from wild and domesticated pigs, small game, insects, leafy greens, bananas, root crops such as cassava and taro, fruits, and nuts.

Preparing sago starch was the main work activity of the women. They cut, scraped, pounded, and washed the pith of the palm to extract the starch, carrying it home in big pinkish-white blocks wrapped in leaves. Most of the sago palms were of seedless varieties that must have at one time, perhaps centuries earlier, been planted from cuttings. These grew on higher ground near the edge of the swamp forest, regenerating the stand by sending up suckers at the base of each palm. Later, when I worked with three geographers on a book about sago, we subtitled it "a tropical starch from marginal lands" to stress how exquisitely adapted a crop it was for wetlands like these (Ruddle et al. 1978).

Wild sago palms with seeds and narrow trunks grew in the depths of the swamp. They could be felled to grow delicious fat grubs, the larvae of beetles that lay their eggs in the fallen log. It was possible to process wild sago for starch, though not in the quantity produced by the domesticated varieties. For all practical purposes, the Saniyo were foragers rather than farmers, seldom needing to plant anything other than bananas and tobacco.

Besides the role of sago in subsistence, another major issue that interested me in the field was *population* growth or decline. Infant and early-childhood mortality was very high, with just over half of the children surviving the first few years of life. The shortage of suitable weaning foods increased the children's vulnerability to infectious disease, though we rarely saw severe malnutrition. Malaria and respiratory diseases such as pneumonia, bronchitis, and tuberculosis were common causes of illness and death. The population was barely replacing itself with this high death rate. Fertility was not very high either. A woman who lived past the age of 50 gave birth on average to five children, but many women died young, before the end of their potential childbearing years.

High mortality is not something that the people ever took for granted—they sought an explanation for every serious illness or death. The death of a child or an old person was attributed to one of several spirits. Some of these were the spirits of the recently dead or more remote ancestors. Some were spirits associated with features of the landscape: a large ironwood tree, a certain vine, or a whirlpool. Such spirit beliefs helped to underwrite a certain attitude of respect for the environment. For example, my neighbors cautioned me not to laugh or speak loudly during an earth tremor or it might become a big earthquake.

If an adult died suddenly in the prime of life, people claimed that a witch was responsible. The local concept of a witch is someone who has eaten human flesh and acquired a taste for it. Witches consume other things that normal people wouldn't eat—earthworms, millipedes, and other repulsive creatures—and eat them through the nose and other orifices. Witches violate food taboos such as the severe ones imposed on widows and widowers. At first, after the death of a spouse, the bereaved could eat hardly anything, only a few bitter wild yams. Gradually vegetable foods were allowed, but most meat remained forbidden for years. Some widows in our village could eat only the meat of rats with their sago. The Saniyo characterized a witch by his or her illegitimate, greedy consumption in violation of food taboos. Fear of witches persisted when we returned in the 1980s, though Christian faith and worship had replaced concern about lesser spirits.

The high mortality experienced by the people we lived with, as in other parts of Papua New Guinea out of the reach of regular health services, reflected, in part, the effects of epidemic diseases such as influenza and whooping cough that swept through the area every few years. The spread of new epidemic diseases was one of the first ways that the Saniyo experienced the expansion of the global economic *system*. In addition to epidemic disease, some plants that came from the Americas, such as tobacco and a seed used for its red pigment (*Bixa orellana*), also came into the area ahead of direct contact with Europeans. Many new food plants arrived (squash, papayas, pineapples, lemons), as well as new animals (cats, chickens). Tilapia, a large African species of fish, was introduced into the Sepik River and worked its way up the tributaries.

Arriving five years after the first colonial Australian patrol, we were there to witness a time of rapid expansion of the world economic system into the area (Townsend and Townsend 2018). Steel axes and knives were replacing stone, shell, and bamboo. Used cotton and polyester clothing was being traded into the area, replacing scratchy grass skirts. A few men went out to coastal plantations to sell their labor. Oil and mineral companies began exploration. They found gold and copper prospects nearby in the 1960s, but low mineral prices and low ore grades made it unprofitable to consider mining them immediately. In 2016, an Australian-based company owned by Chinese investors submitted a plan to dig the nearby Frieda Mine. They proposed building a pipeline and road that will run directly through these villages and totally upend the sustainable way of life we had encountered.

THE FIELD OF ANTHROPOLOGY

The research that I did in Papua New Guinea is called ethnographic fieldwork and the written results are called *ethnography*, quite literally "writing about people," or, the scientific description of a culture. This kind of ethnographic fieldwork is sometimes done by sociologists and geographers as well as anthropologists. Increasingly it is recognized that ethnography is a project of collaboration between an ethnographer and the community members. This is clearly seen in a work like *Landscape Traveled by Coyote and Crane* (Frey 2001). In it the Schitsu'umsh (Coeur d'Alene Indian) storytellers, singers, and actors in ceremonials portrayed the way they viewed their landscape.

The ethnographic work was done in part to document the impact of environmental degradation from mining and smelting in Idaho's Silver Valley for the Tribe's Natural Resource Damage Assessment.

Rather than settling down in a single village, many of today's ethnographers must engage in *multisited ethnography*. In her research on nature conservation in postsocialist Bulgaria, Barbara Cellarius began her research in a village of 700 in the Rhodope Mountains, on the southern border of Bulgaria and Greece, learning about villagers' gathering of mushrooms and other forest products, potato farming, and livestock keeping. Subsequently she did fieldwork in the regional center and in Sofia, the national capital, researching environmental organizations. Later she visited the headquarters in England and Switzerland of international organizations, such as the WWF and the Royal Society for the Protection of Birds, environmental organizations with projects in Bulgaria (Cellarius 2004). Following her research in Bulgaria, Cellarius returned to the United States and became park anthropologist for a national park in Alaska.

When I introduce myself as an anthropologist, people invariably say, "Oh, how interesting, you study old bones and stones," and I mumble, "No, I'm a *cultural* anthropologist. I study *living* people." But they are not far off the mark in naming two of the main subfields of anthropology. The "bones" as well as flesh, blood, and genes refer to **biological anthropology**, also called physical anthropology or human biology. The "stones" refer to *prehistoric* **archaeology**, the study of the material remains of past cultures. The fourth traditional subfield is *anthropological linguistics*. A strong training in linguistics was especially important for me because I was going to a place that was a big blank on the language map of the world at that time. A fieldworker who planned to go to Japan, for example, would find already-existing grammars, dictionaries, and language courses allowing language learning before going to the field, which was not possible for me.

To the traditional four subfields of anthropology, there is sometimes added a fifth, **applied anthropology**. Others simply regard applied anthropology as a dimension of all the subfields, that is, any use of anthropology to solve practical problems. This is what I have done for much of my career, for example, studying health service delivery in Papua New Guinea from 1980 to 1984. Later I directed a church-related agency that resettled Kurdish, Sudanese, Eastern European, and other refugees in Buffalo, New York. Then I did work on the role of churches and interfaith coalitions in the communities surrounding Superfund sites and their role in identifying hazards, communicating risk, and remediating these hazardous waste sites. The Superfund is a federal program of the U.S. Environmental Protection Agency for cleaning up the nation's most seriously chemically contaminated sites. Since retirement, I have combined climate justice activism with informal research on how religious organizations have responded to the climate crisis.

Threaded through all the subfields of anthropology is ***environmental anthropology***, the topic of this book. My own training is largely in ***cultural anthropology***, so the fieldwork I did in Papua New Guinea and later in Superfund communities illustrates how a cultural anthropologist goes about studying environmental issues using the methods of ethnography—interviewing and observing people's behavior. An archaeologist uses quite different methods, digging up the evidence of human impact on ancient environments. Archaeologists collaborate with specialized zooarchaeologists, archaeobotanists, and geoarchaeologists to understand the animal and plant remains and the soils that they have excavated. One of the most imaginative uses of archaeological methods is the University of Arizona's Garbage Project (Rathje and Murphy 1992). Archaeology students sorted bags of household garbage. Later they also excavated landfills. Initially intended merely to teach archaeological techniques, the project gave unusual insight into our culture's patterns of consumption, waste, and recycling. For one thing, they discovered by sorting the hazardous wastes in household garbage that people throw out a lot more household cleaners and pesticides than they admit to.

Ideally, the several subfields of anthropology work together to produce a holistic account of human nature. In practice, this is often difficult to achieve, though collaboration sometimes occurs, as in the following case of ethnoprimatology. A biological anthropologist, Melissa Remis, studied lowland gorillas while her cultural anthropologist colleague Rebecca Hardin studied hunting-gathering humans, the Baka, in the same forest reserve in Central African Republic. Together they documented the impact of logging, roads, and a growing trade in bush meat on the depletion of wildlife populations. Even in the core of the park, where conservation activities should have protected them, there were fewer gorillas, elephants, and duikers as the human presence increased (Hardin and Remis 2006). In subsequent chapters of this book there will be examples of environmental anthropology that draw on all the subfields of anthropology.

ORGANIZATION OF THIS BOOK

This book will follow a somewhat historical path through the first several chapters, although it is not intended to give a full-fledged history of environmental anthropology. Chapter 2 picks up the history of the field in the late 1940s and early 1950s, when Julian Steward introduced the concept of ***cultural ecology*** into anthropology. Chapter 3 moves on to the early 1960s when much of the excitement in environmental anthropology surrounded *ethnobiology*, a new approach to field-work that drew mostly on **linguistics** to study the traditional knowledge that people had about plants, animals, and other aspects of the environment. Chapters 4, 5, and 6 are concerned with work that started in the 1960s and 1970s and brought concepts and methods into anthropology from outside the discipline, primarily from general ecology as practiced by biologists. Chapter 4 highlights the work of Roy Rappaport in Papua New Guinea and Chapter 5 the work of several anthropologists in the Amazon region. This research in small tropical forest communities is balanced in Chapter 6 by looking at the ways that ecological anthropologists approach larger agricultural populations in complex societies. This chapter refers to classic studies by well-known anthropologists such as Fredrik Barth, Clifford Geertz, and the late Robert Netting and Eric Wolf. Throughout this roughly historical overview, in Chapters 2 through 6, I emphasize that many of the ideas and approaches developed earlier continue to be useful in the present, contributing to understanding the ways that present-day local populations of human beings adapt to their physical and biological environments.

The later chapters explore the interaction between the local and the global that preoccupies environmental anthropologists today. Chapter 7 tells about the social and environmental impact of an open-pit copper and gold mine. While this one happens to be in Papua New Guinea, the multinational corporation that owned it also operated mines in Australia, Canada, and Chile. A completely new Chapter 8 looks at the impact of war on the environment. Chapter 9 explores hazards, especially those stemming from global climate change. Chapter 10 considers world population from the viewpoint provided by anthropology, while Chapter 11 looks at the loss of **biodiversity** and its implications for human health. Chapter 12 describes the work of applied anthropologists on practical problems of conservation. Chapter 13 explores the way in which the religions of the world view the environment and the protection they afford to sacred places. Chapter 14, the concluding chapter, talks about personal engagement with environmental problems including lifestyle choices and their implications for the environment.

RECOMMENDED READING

Michael R. Dove and Carol Carpenter, eds. 2008. *Environmental Anthropology: A Historical Reader*. Malden, MA: Blackwell Pub. Twenty-four classic articles in this reader complement the first several chapters of this textbook.

Carl A. Zimring and William L Rathje, eds. 2012. *Encyclopedia of Consumption and Waste: The Social Science of Garbage*. Thousand Oaks, CA: SAGE Reference. 2 vols. Encyclopedic coverage of "garbology" with entries from "acid rain" to "zero waste," including states and countries.

Chapter Two

Julian Steward's Cultural Ecology

N o species thrives in such a wide range of environments as Homo sapiens. Spreading out, often at the expense of other animals and plants, we humans have come to occupy lands with a wide range of latitude and altitude, with varying physical characteristics and rainfall. From fossil remains several million years old, physical anthropologists infer that we emerged in a subtropical African savanna, a landscape of mixed trees and grassland. From there we have gone on to inhabit deserts, tropical and temperate forests, high altitudes above the tree line, and most recently the most extreme Arctic environments. We have even visited outer space and deep undersea environments.

The adaptations that made it possible for humans to spread so widely have not been genetic ones, for the most part. We remain a single, interbreeding species with relatively minor differences among us to show for our ancestors' experience with environmental extremes. Pale, lightly pigmented skin, for example, is an adaptation that allowed people to avoid vitamin D deficiencies (the crooked bones of rickets) in northern environments lacking adequate sunshine. The cost of this adaptation was an increased susceptibility to skin cancer after light-skinned people again migrated to sunny climates like Australia and California. Similarly, the sickle cell trait and certain other variants of hemoglobin are genetic adaptations that offer some protection against malaria. They offer survival advantage only in places where the parasites that cause malaria and the mosquitoes that transmit it are part of the environment.

The adaptations that allow Homo sapiens to thrive in many different environments are largely behavioral rather than genetic. We build and live in houses suitable to the climate, put on or take off clothing in response to weather conditions, and make and use tools that are efficient for capturing whatever other species are available and desirable for food. Most of these behavioral adaptations are socially learned; that is, they are cultural. When taking this adaptive perspective, anthropologists view cultures as intimately related to the physical and biological environments in which they occur. A culture is a way of life, a tool kit for survival in a particular place and time on the planet.

A SHORT HISTORY OF
ENVIRONMENTAL ANTHROPOLOGY

Environmental perspectives go back a long way in the history of anthropology, but they have had their ups and downs. In some eras, anthropologists have been very interested in the environment; at other times, they tended to contemplate culture as a thing in itself, like a beautiful vase on display or a written text to be translated or interpreted without much reference to its environment. In this short book, we will not look back farther than the middle of the twentieth century, when Julian Steward introduced the idea of cultural ecology. Steward's cultural ecology gathered adherents and then was transformed into ecological anthropology. This transformation came in part from adopting the concept of the ecosystem from biology.

Ecological anthropology got a big boost from developments in the wider societies of the United States and Europe in the 1970s. The first Earth Day celebration, April 22, 1970, mobilized 20 million Americans in peaceful demonstrations. In 1973 and 1979, waiting in long lines at gasoline pumps, many people worried that population growth and economic development would outrun the supply of petroleum and other nonrenewable resources. Also in the late 1970s the publicity surrounding toxic industrial wastes at sites such as Love Canal made it clear that hazardous wastes could not simply be buried and forgotten. The dangers of pesticides that Rachel Carson had publicized in her book *Silent Spring* (Carson 1962) were not limited to birds. With public interest in environmental issues at a peak, the 1970s were a high point of research in ecological anthropology, though this interest slacked off in the 1980s. These were the Reagan years, when much of the environmental legislation passed in the 1970s was weakened by deregulation and lack of enforcement.

By the 1990s, environmental anthropology was again at the forefront. As always, developments in the academic disciplines paralleled those in the wider public. The United Nations Conference on Environment and Development held in Rio de Janeiro, Brazil, in 1992 drew public attention to issues such as deforestation and the loss of biological diversity. Another United Nations conference in Kyoto, Japan, in 1997 gave voice to concerns about global climate change. In the American Anthropological Association, the major scholarly and professional organization for the discipline, a new section called Anthropology and Environment was organized (Crumley 2001). Several graduate departments established programs with concentrations in environmental anthropology. Most importantly, environmental anthropology was no longer just an academic discipline, discussed in university classrooms. The conversations now included many practitioners—applied environmental anthropologists working in government agencies, nongovernment organizations (NGOs), and businesses.

Anthropologists' involvement with environmental issues has become more differentiated, with a wide variety of methods, theories, and specialized research interests. Anthropologists using these newer approaches might identify themselves as evolutionary ecologists, historical ecologists, political ecologists, or ethnoecologists. In this text, I use the term environmental anthropology as an umbrella for these approaches.

Some anthropologists use the term ecological anthropology for what I have called environmental anthropology, but I use ecological anthropology in a somewhat narrower sense. Ecological anthropology will refer to one type of research in environmental anthropology—field studies that describe ecosystems that include a human population. Studies in ecological anthropology often deal with a small population of only a few hundred people, such as a village or neighborhood. The disadvantage of both terms is that they emphasize anthropology as the larger discipline of which they are a part. Over the years, I have found that my concerns are just as often addressed by as many geographers as anthropologists; all of us might call ourselves "political ecologists" or "cultural ecologists" to downplay the differences in academic affiliation.

THE CULTURAL ECOLOGY OF JULIAN STEWARD

More than any other anthropologist, Julian Steward was responsible for the development of environmental anthropology, particularly in the years he spent at Columbia University in the late 1940s and early 1950s, where he influenced an important generation of anthropologists with his theory of cultural ecology and evolution. Steward had started his career at the University of California in the 1930s. At that time, he made several trips throughout the Great Basin area of Nevada, Utah, and parts of neighboring states, visiting the Western Shoshoni and their Paiute and Ute neighbors.

By the time Steward did his survey, the indigenous societies of the Great Basin had been drastically affected by the intrusion of miners and ranchers. Grazing sheep and cattle had reduced the wild seeds that had been the mainstay of the traditional Native diet. Large game had always been scarce in this area, though occasionally deer, mountain sheep, bison, or antelope could be killed. Rabbits and other small game were more significant. The plant life determined the seasonal migrations of Great Basin people—greens in spring, ripening seeds in early summer, edible roots and berries in late summer, and pine nuts in the fall.

After their nineteenth-century wars with the settlers, the Indians left their old system of subsistence based on foraging on the land to work on ranches or in mines and towns. Because of this change, Steward could not do intensive fieldwork to observe ongoing subsistence activities, that is, the kind of fieldwork described later in this book. Steward patched together nineteenth-century descriptions and censuses, his own plant collections and environmental observations, and data he collected by interviewing Indians, such as their lists of the names and uses of plants.

During the presettler period, most of the subsistence activities of the Shoshonean Indians were carried out by one or two families moving about this dry, sparsely populated area to forage for plant foods and small game. Only in the winter could they camp with 20 or 30 families living close enough to visit each other.

Steward rejected the notion, prevalent in his time, that the culture of the Shoshoni could be explained only by tracing historical links to earlier cultures. While he agreed that their material culture—baskets, pots, and tools—was mostly derived from the Southwest, he considered that their economic and social organization was the result of using that technology to exploit the unpredictable environment of the arid Great Basin. Steward defined the "cultural core" as the features of social and economic life that are most closely related to subsistence (Steward 1955). In approaching a new culture, Steward said, it is not possible to know what is the cultural core in advance, but by using the *method of cultural ecology* one can determine this. First, anthropologists analyze the relationship of the technology used in production to the natural resources exploited. Then they relate other behavioral patterns to subsistence. For example, do people work alone or cooperatively? Finally, they can ask how these patterns of subsisting in the environment affect other aspects of the culture, such as kinship or religion.

EVOLUTION IN CULTURAL ANTHROPOLOGY

Steward's method of cultural ecology was part of a more general move to reintroduce the concept of cultural evolution to anthropology. Nineteenth-century anthropologists such as Lewis Henry Morgan and E. B. Tylor had advocated the view that all cultures evolved through a similar series of stages from simple to complex. American anthropology in the early twentieth century unfolded in reaction to this view. This reaction took the form of *cultural relativism*. Each culture was accepted on its own terms as a product of its unique history. Attempts to find general laws or causal explanations were regarded with suspicion. Steward disagreed, arguing that there were regularities to be discerned in the way that cultures change. It was the job of anthropology to determine these cause and effect sequences through empirical study, that is, scientific research based on observation and comparison. These sequences of change were not universal; hence Steward used the term *multilinear* evolution in contrast to the *unilinear* evolution of nineteenth-century anthropology.

Many of Steward's followers picked up the concept of multilinear evolution, but generally they called it by other names. Elman Service and Marshall Sahlins distinguished two processes of cultural evolution—general and specific. General evolution was an increase in scale and complexity, a concept emphasized by their colleague and mentor Leslie White (1959). Specific evolution was the equivalent of Steward's multilinear evolution and came to be called "cultural adaptation" (Sahlins, Service, and Harding 1960).

Of course, not all cultural practices are environmental adaptations, and some are outright *mal*adaptive. Consider for example the American preoccupation with grass front lawns at the cost of increased use of chemical fertilizers, herbicides, and insecticides. The runoff from lawns added to that from **agriculture** contributes to water pollution. It also threatens the health of children and pets. Product marketing efforts and suburban neighborhood pressures promote an aesthetic standard that is counter to the common good (Robbins and Sharp 2003).

Rather than concentrating on the *outcome* of adaptation, it may be more helpful to concentrate on the *process* of adaptation, accepting that the outcome may not always be favorable (*mal*adaptation). Cultural ecologists who follow in Steward's path today look at the way societies respond to changes in their environment and in the cultural core.

CULTURAL ECOLOGY AND
THE LAST NORTHERN COD

A contemporary example of cultural ecology comes from the Canadian fishing industry. The northern cod (*Gadus morhua*) became so scarce in the Atlantic waters off Newfoundland that the fisheries management officials had to declare a moratorium on fishing in 1992. When the cod-fishing industry collapsed, thousands of fishing crews and plant workers lost their jobs. Most social scientists tried to explain this collapse by reference to economic and political factors. One of the anthropologists who analyzed the catastrophe found that the more important thing to understand was the relationship of specific aspects of fishing technology (i.e., Steward's culture core) and environment (McGuire 1997).

Foreign factory freezer trawlers from many European countries began fishing intensively in the waters off Newfoundland in the 1960s. Regulation of their catch was ineffective, and the catch declined steeply from a peak of 800,000 tons in 1968 to about one-quarter of that in 1976. In 1977 Canada barred the foreign fleets, declaring exclusive control over its coastal waters in a 200-mile zone. The Fisheries Department took on regulation of the industry. They limited fishing by issuing fishing licenses and keeping the total catch at a level set by the best scientific knowledge available. Unfortunately, the method for assessing catches turned out to be flawed. By turning to the "hard" sciences, the fisheries agency ignored the local knowledge of inshore fishing crews. The crews had already picked up danger signals that the fish stock was in trouble in the 1980s, when they had to work harder to catch smaller fish than previously.

Changes in the technology of fishing accompanied the declining catch. Increasingly the Canadian crews used Japanese cod traps, roofed fish traps with smaller mesh that could be used in areas with rough bottoms. These traps captured the smaller, younger fish. Other new technology included echo sounders and advanced navigation equipment. These changes in technology made it possible to catch "the last northern cod." In 2003, the Canadian Minister of Fisheries and Oceans closed all commercial and recreational fishing for the northern cod in eastern Newfoundland and the Gulf of St. Lawrence. Subsequently, limited fishing was permitted. In the 1990s, it appeared that the cod might even become extinct, but fish stocks began to recover. Meanwhile, fishermen had adapted to changed conditions and had begun specializing in crab and shrimp, species that flourished with the decline of the predatory cod (Davis 2014).

As the northern cod example shows, Steward's approach continues to be useful. Many anthropologists and geographers continue to identify themselves as cultural ecologists, regarding culture and ecology as equally significant (Anderson 1996; Netting 1986). Even so, cultural ecology branched almost immediately into one wing of anthropologists who put more emphasis on the "cultural" (chapter 3) and another wing who put more emphasis on the "ecology" (chapters 4 and 5). The latter identified individuals or populations, not cultures, as the adaptive units that respond to the environment and form the basic units of the ecosystem and argued that human *behavior*, rather than culture, should be the focus of analysis.

RECOMMENDED READING

Engagement. A blog published by the Anthropology and Environment Society, a section of the American Anthropological Association. Firsthand anthropological accounts of current issues related to social and ecological justice. https://aesengagement.wordpress.com/; on Twitter: @Engaged_EAnthro

Robert McC. Netting. 1986. *Cultural Ecology*, 2nd ed. Long Grove, IL: Waveland Press. The short classic textbook introducing this perspective, by an anthropologist with field experience in Nigeria and Switzerland.

RECOMMENDED FILM

Pew Charitable Trusts. New England Ocean Conservation. 2011. *Cod: The Fish That Made New England*. 4 minutes. Old-timers in New England's cod fishery tell and show how it used to be. http://www.pewtrusts.org/en/projects/new-england-ocean-conservation

Chapter Three

Ethnoecology

Culture has long been the key concept in American anthropology, and it has almost as many definitions as there are anthropologists, though these definitions share many common features. One definition is: "Culture is what one must know to act effectively in one's environment" (Hunn 1989), where the word *environment* has both natural and social components. The environment is seen from the point of view of an individual actor. The focus is on culture as a system of knowledge or a set of rules for behavior, that is, on the ***cognitive*** aspects of culture. A deliberate ambiguity in the quoted definition is the word *effectively*. Who is to judge what is effective? An insider (a native of the culture), an outsider (the scientist), or the impersonal process of natural selection that weeds out the unsuccessful? It may be that these will coincide most of the time, as individuals pursue cultural goals that also lead to survival of the biological species.

Observations of the environment may lead to useful conclusions even if they are embedded in very different worldviews. For example, Aymara and Quechua farmers in the central Andes use an ancient method to forecast rainfall and potato crop yields several months in advance by observing the apparent brightness of the star cluster Pleiades during the month of June. They use these weather forecasts to adjust planting dates. The anthropologist reporting this information discovered that high cirrus cloud cover causes poor visibility of these stars in El Niño years, when less rain falls during the growing season (Orlove, Chiang, and Cane 2000).

One whole branch of environmental anthropology has followed the path suggested by the cognitive definition of culture, developing increasingly sophisticated studies of cultural knowledge. Cognitive anthropologists developed their methods by studying small, closed sets of terms such as the words for colors or kinship relations. Each of these sets of terms is called a ***semantic domain***, that is, an area of meaning in a language. The studies that are most relevant to environmental anthropology are studies of ethnotaxonomy, that is, the way that people name and classify plants and animals, and studies of ethnobiology, the full range of their knowledge about plants and animals.

THE STUDY OF TRADITIONAL
ENVIRONMENTAL KNOWLEDGE

Ethnobiology is not just a matter of matching up scientific labels to the local language names but also of understanding what features of the plants or animals that people attend to in classifying them as they do. These may be quite different from what scientists emphasize. From these categories, the ethnoscientist moves on to understanding the cultural rules for using them—recognizing what reeds and palm woods are useful for making arrows of specific types for hunting birds, mammals, or other game, for example. Ultimately the ethnoscientist seeks to understand how people make complex decisions such as where to clear a field and when to plant, weed, and harvest.

Speakers of the Sahaptin language along the Columbia River of Washington and Oregon use 26 recorded words for different kinds of roots, *xni-t*, "plants that are dug" (Hunn and Selam 1990). Most of the 26 different named types of roots correspond to biological species as scientists classify them. But at the next step up in hierarchy of the Sahaptin classification, the more general ethnobotanical category "roots" includes members of several plant families. Some of the roots belong to the family Umbelliferae, a large botanical family that includes familiar plants such as carrots, parsley, and celery. Others, including the Sahaptin staple food, the camas, belong to the Liliaceae, the family that includes onions and garlic as well as lilies. These "roots" are closely related, from a botanist's point of view, to other plants that Sahaptin speakers know to be inedible or even poisonous. Despite the botanical similarities, the Sahaptin do not include the inedible plants in their category *xni-t*.

Columbia River Indian elder James Selam and his extended family taught their rich cultural knowledge of the environment to anthropologist Eugene Hunn. Among the hundreds of plants and animals documented, the roots had been particularly important in their ancestors' diet, along with salmon and venison. This knowledge was valued and retained by some modern-day Sahaptins, although their lives and diets were much changed by the establishment of reservations and the building of hydroelectric dams along the Columbia. Hunn's work with James Selam on roots is a good illustration of **_ethnoecology_**. The pioneer of this field was Harold Conklin (1954), who described the knowledge required by the Hanunóo of the Philippines to farm the tropical forests. Other early ethnoecologists include anthropologist Ralph Bulmer and his Kalam collaborator Saem Majnep who gained respect for work on New Guinea birds as did Brent Berlin and his colleagues for work on Tzeltal plants in southern Mexico.

As ethnoecologists completed studies of numerous folk classification systems, it became possible to reach conclusions based on the comparison of more than one such system. This method can be used, for example, to address the question of differences between foragers and farmers in their knowledge of the environment, as it is reflected in their botanical terminology. The Guajá and the Ka'apor both live in the eastern part of Brazilian Amazonia. They inhabit the same botanical habitat and speak closely related languages. Yet the Ka'apor, who are farmers, have many more botanical terms than the Guajá, who are foragers. This difference reflects the fact that the Ka'apor not only have more terms for cultivated plants, they also have many more differentiated terms for kinds of wild plants, about five times as many. How can this be? As farmers the Ka'apor are familiar with the kinds of trees that they cut out of tropical forests to make their gardens. Their gardens create light gaps that create a biologically diverse habitat. When their crops fail, they are prepared to forage for wild plants, too. For all these reasons they have developed and preserved an even richer botanical vocabulary than their Guajá neighbors (Balée 1999).

An important achievement of ethnoecological studies is that they bring recognition to the traditional environmental knowledge (TEK) of indigenous peoples, who often are ethnic minorities held in contempt by the majority populations of their country. Their subsistence systems are often criticized, too, by outsiders who see them as backward and who covet their land for raising cash crops, for farming more intensively, or even for establishing national parks. Ethnoecological studies show that TEK is a body of knowledge that is extensive, observationally grounded, and complementary to scientific knowledge. Increasingly, policy makers have attempted to incorporate TEK into their work. Ethnoecologists showed how TEK could be used to design programs of economic development that would not be environmentally destructive, such as the gathering of tree resins in the forests of Indonesian Borneo (Donovan and Puri 2004).

Only recently has traditional environmental knowledge begun to be accorded formal respect by those making environmental policy, and it has not often been put to practical use, even in countries that were committed to do so (Hernández-Morcillo, et al. 2014). In the work of the Millennium Ecosystem Assessment, scientists struggled to find ways to take the local knowledge of indigenous people into account in reporting the current state of our living planet (Brosius 2006). Tragically, these systems of traditional environmental knowledge are threatened not only by the loss of lands but also by the loss of the languages that encode them. At least one third of the world's 7,099 languages are threatened. Thirteen percent are dying, that is, they are spoken only by old people, and children are not learning them; instead they are learning national or trade languages (Simons and Fennig 2017). Areas with high linguistic and cultural diversity also tend to be areas with high biodiversity, which is threatened by many of the same forces.

Hence, efforts to protect the environment are increasingly linked to work for the human rights of indigenous peoples (Maffí 2005).

ETHNOECOLOGY AND LANDSCAPE

While much of TEK is encoded in language, other parts of this knowledge are acquired experientially, through practice. Leslie Main Johnson (2010) found this to be true of the Gitksan and other First Nations that she lived among in northwestern Canada. The elders taught her a great deal as she studied plants used as food and medicine. It would be possible to conduct a study simply of the plant terms in their language, but to understand the context one needs to get out on the Land. "Land," for the First Nations, like "Country" for Australian Aborigines, is more than just a territory. As hunters, fisherfolk, and gatherers of roots and berries the Gitksan move through the Land year-round on foot, by canoe, or by snowmobile; they therefore speak of it more in terms of trails than of fields. They have a rich language of place names and kinds of places that reflects the rivers and lakes, land formations, vegetation cover, kinds of animals hunted there, such as beavers or mountain goats, and events that have happened there. Land includes social and political relationships and a spiritual dimension.

Johnson and others refer to this whole complex as *landscape ethnoecology*. **Landscape** has different meanings in different disciplines. For geographers and ecologists, a landscape is a unit that includes more than one ecosystem and the land on which it is found. By speaking of landscape *ethnoecology* anthropologists emphasize that humans are part of the landscape and the land is viewed anthropocentrically, including their knowledge systems and their relationships to nonhuman beings whether plants, animals, or spirits.

NATURE AND CULTURE:
A UNIVERSAL DICHOTOMY?

Underlying our discussion of folk taxonomies was an unstated assumption that there is something called "nature" in contrast to "culture." Nature is "out there" and consists of the biotic and abiotic (living and nonliving) environment. Culture is "in here," in the human mind, but we can find out about it by asking the right questions and observing behavior. This seems to imply that there is a hierarchical relationship between culture and nature in which culture imposes order on nature or discovers order that is already in nature.

The nature:culture distinction once was unquestioned. The French anthropologist Claude Lévi-Strauss saw it as a universal structure, hardwired in the human brain. From the binary contrast between nature and culture, Lévi-Strauss thought that other metaphorical contrasts followed logically, such as the dichotomy between wild and tame, raw and cooked, and female and male.

This assertion that women were associated with nature and men with culture led feminist anthropologists to question the assumption that the distinction between nature and culture was universal (MacCormack and Strathern 1980). MacCormack's work in Africa and Strathern's in New Guinea led them to suggest that the concept of "nature" was ethnocentric, that is, that Europeans and Americans simply were imposing their own ideas about nature on other people. Other cultures did not have the same idea of nature or the metaphors that were said to follow from it. Other cultures did not separate the cultural from the natural. Even if they did make that separation, they constructed the boundaries between them differently than Westerners did. After the feminist anthropologists opened up this topic of nature and culture, anthropologists continued to debate it fervently.

In the 1990s, it became common for anthropologists to say that nature is "socially constructed." By this they did not mean that there was no biophysical reality or that it was all in our (collective) heads. They did insist that the language we use about nature does not mirror an essential reality out there but brings it into being and shapes it into a social reality. Different cultures use different symbols or metaphors in talking about nature; for example, many foraging people describe the forest as a parent, giving them sustenance. Many hunting peoples describe hunting as a form of exchange in which animals-as-persons give themselves to the hunter. Scientists in the electronic era, including ecological anthropologists, often described the human environment with analogies such as thermostats and computer programs, regulating them within boundaries. Talking about nature is not just a matter for linguists to analyze but also raises questions of power, of who has the authority to speak (Escobar 1998).

The next step in this discussion within anthropology is referred to as "the ontological turn," from the philosophical term ontology, which means, roughly, the question or study of what sorts of things exist. Some ethnographers argued that different cultures do not simply describe the world differently, they live in different worlds in which recognition as persons may be extended to animals and to other kinds of living entities that Western culture would assign to the category "supernatural." This theoretical development was at least partly related to the sharpened awareness in the early twenty-first century that we are living in a time of ecological crisis, a new epoch characterized by human-caused global climate change and massive species extinctions. The new theoretical development was stimulated by French scholars including Bruno Latour and Philippe Descola and

Americanist anthropologists working in the Amazon, including Brazilian Eduardo Vivieros de Castro.

How Forests Think is one of the catchiest titles among the works produced by the ontological turn in anthropology. In this book, Eduardo Kohn (2013) writes of the Runa people of his native Ecuador. By telling us about Runa understandings of the relationship between trees, monkeys, and Runa hunters or Runa shamans and jaguars, he shows us that culture and nature are part of a single system to which living beings other than humans actively contribute meanings.

Whether or not they align themselves with the topic of ontology, many anthropologists have taken a step away from anthropocentrism to center their ethnographies on nonhuman species from microbes or mushrooms to dogs or elephants. Since interactions with humans are part of the story, their fieldwork and writing is called *multispecies ethnography*.

RECOMMENDED READING

E. N. Anderson, Deborah Pearsall, Eugene Hunn, and Nancy Turner, eds. 2011. *Ethnobiology*. Hoboken, NJ: John Wiley & Sons, Inc. The definitive review of the field, written by leading members of the Society for Ethnobiology.

Society for Ethnobiology. *Forage!* The blog is one of several ways in which the Society publishes its work, including even a light-hearted look at the top 10 ethnobiology tattoos. https://ethnobiology.org/forage/blog

RECOMMENDED FILMS

UAMuseumOfTheNorth. 2016. *Ties to Alaska's Wild Plants*. University of Alaska. A playlist of 9 short films about plants used in the indigenous cultures of Alaska. https://www.youtube.com/user/UAMuseumOfTheNorth/playlists

Chapter Four

Pigs for the Ancestors

As their pig herd increased in size, quarrels erupted among the Tsembaga Maring of the mountainous interior of Papua New Guinea. Pigs foraging in the tropical forest occasionally broke through a fence into a garden and uprooted sweet potatoes and yams. Women began to grumble about the extra work they had to do feeding the pigs, now that there were too many pigs to get along on just sweet potato peelings and leftovers: by June 1962, the pigs numbered 162. There were almost as many pigs as there were people; the population of the Tsembaga local group was 200.

The Tsembaga reached the consensus that it was time to hold a *kaiko*, a yearlong festival that would culminate in a huge feast at which most of the pigs would be sacrificed, leaving only 60 juvenile pigs by the end of 1963. The goal of the rituals was to increase the fertility and growth of people and their gardens and pigs. The pigs slaughtered in the rituals are dedicated to various spirits, particularly the spirits of deceased ancestors. Prior to the peace enforced by the Australian colonial government, the ritual cycle was integrated with the cycle of war and peace among Maring local groups.

During the year that the kaiko was held, Roy A. Rappaport and his wife, Ann, were resident with the Tsembaga. They observed the rituals as well as the routine of daily life. Rappaport was at the time a PhD student at Columbia University. As part of his dissertation research project he weighed all the food eaten by the Tomegai, a Tsembaga clan consisting of the people cooking and eating at four fireplaces: ten adults, one adolescent, and five children. He also measured their gardens and observed gardening practices. He found that the main starchy staples that they grew—taro, sweet potato, yam, and banana—comprised more than half of the Tsembaga diet. Meat provided only about 1 percent of the normal day-to-day food. Even so, the Tsembaga diet was less monotonous than others reported from Highland New Guinea. Abundant greens, pandanus palm fruits, and sugarcane added variety. Except for sweet potato, a relatively recent introduction from South America, all these crops were domesticated in New Guinea. Archaeologists have established that agriculture arose independently in Highland New Guinea, possibly not much later than barley and wheat in the Middle East, rice in China, and maize in Mexico, about 10,000 years ago (Golson et al. 2017).

Though meat played little part in the day-to-day diet of the Tsembaga Maring, this changed radically at the culmination of the kaiko, when enough pigs were killed to provide every Tsembaga man, woman, and child with about 12 pounds of pork. The pork was eaten over a period of five days. In addition, 2,000 to 3,000 other people in neighboring groups received an average of two to three pounds per person. The total was nearly four *tons* of edible meat.

A NEW GUINEA ECOSYSTEM

Like the cultural ecologists who preceded him, Rappaport regarded subsistence as central to his research, though he avoided the concepts of culture and cultural core, preferring to speak of "behavior" to facilitate comparison with the behavior of other animals. He went farther than the cultural ecologists had done in quantifying food and work. These measurements gave him the data needed to describe the flow of energy and materials through the ecosystem. Because he wanted to unify ecological anthropology with general ecology, he intended to use the concept of ecosystem in the same way that a biological ecologist would use it to describe an ecosystem such as a pond or a forest. The ecosystem concept was derived from the work of ecologists such as Eugene Odum, whose 1953 textbook *Fundamentals of Ecology* first promoted the concept widely, though it had been used earlier.

Rappaport considered the Tsembaga territory to be an ecosystem consisting of a population of human beings, local populations of pigs and other animal and plant species, and the nonliving substances such as soil and water on which they all depended. These components were linked into a system by the mutual exchange of matter, energy, and information—from the plants that produced food through photosynthesis to the **bacteria** that decomposed leftover sweet potato peelings.

People are enmeshed with pigs in different ecosystems throughout the world. Tsembaga pigs forage in the forest as well as remain tame through being fed by the women. This pattern differs from the wild pigs hunted by the nomadic Penan in the forest of Borneo (Puri 2005) or, at the opposite extreme, from the industrial pigs raised in concentrated animal feeding operations (CAFOs) of North Carolina or the American Midwest.

Like the biological ecologists of his day, Rappaport employed a **systems theory** approach, treating the Tsembaga ecosystem as a closed **feedback** system in equilibrium with its surroundings. Such a system is self-regulating and sustainable. It was not assumed that the system would be changeless; indeed, it had to change, adapt, or evolve simply to survive in a changing world. The use of systems theory was inspired by the enthusiasm for computer modeling, a leading-edge development at the time, though Rappaport's book (1968) did not itself contain a computer model. Rappaport's work stimulated a huge amount of discussion, reanalysis, and fieldwork by other anthropologists.

CRITIQUES OF RAPPAPORT'S WORK

Nutritionists pointed out that the kaiko, as described by Rappaport, was a very wasteful way to distribute the scarce animal protein available to the Tsembaga. Physiologically, they would have made better use of the protein by slaughtering fewer pigs on more frequent occasions. Of course, Rappaport had not claimed that this was the most efficient use of the meat; he only claimed that the timing of the ritual in coordination with the cycle of war and peace assured that high-quality protein would be available to injured warriors when needed. Nonetheless, this is probably one of the weaker links in his argument, as he himself later admitted (Rappaport 1984:473–478). The core of his argument was not the nutritional advantage but the role that ritual played in regulating the relationships between local groups.

Another set of criticisms that responded to Rappaport's book had to do with the setting of boundaries around an ecosystem, in both space and time. How could Rappaport limit his study to the Tsembaga when they fought and traded with other local groups? This problem is one that biologists face as well. What are the boundaries of a forest or a stream? The scientist sets these boundaries somewhat arbitrarily, but only after considering whether the exchanges within the system are greater than those outside.

Some ecological anthropologists after Rappaport despaired of defining higher-level units such as ecosystems and chose to focus instead on the individual organism interacting with its environment and on the process of natural selection operating on individuals. These anthropologists made their interdisciplinary connections more to evolutionary biology than to ecology. Rather than studying whole ecosystems and assuming that they are self-regulating, they chose to study the payoff of different behavioral strategies adopted by individuals. This approach was most easily applied to studying the strategies adopted by hunters (Alvard 1995; Winterhalder 2001). This kind of work is called human evolutionary ecology or human behavioral ecology.

Other ecological anthropologists chose to move in the opposite direction, toward studying larger, more inclusive units rather than local populations. This led them to analyze whole regions such as Amazonia, empires referred to as *world systems*, and ultimately global studies of the entire planet, the "ecosphere" (Hornborg and Crumley 2007; Hornborg et al. 2007).

Setting limits of time is just as tricky as setting limits of space. Rappaport's study was based on data from a field study of a little more than a year and on people's memories of a generation or two. Tsembaga Maring ritual is assumed to work as a homeostat: Through negative feedback it returns the system to stability when it threatens to get out of balance. (For comparison, think of a thermostat that switches a furnace off and on to keep the room temperature within comfortable limits.)

Taking a longer view, we ask: How did this system of ritual regulation come to be? How can we allow for change and evolution? In the years just after Rappaport's study, cultural anthropology in general moved into a phase of great interest in history. Ecological anthropologists also began to accommodate long historical time frames and environmental transformations. This approach came to be known as *historical ecology* (Crumley 1993).

Rappaport wanted to link ecological anthropology to general ecology. In doing so, he linked it to the ecology of his day, but ecology as a science was changing, too. Ecology began to move away from the emphasis on *equilibrium* that Rappaport had picked up; the titles of publications began to use words like "chaos," "discord," and "surprise." Many scientific disciplines in addition to ecology moved toward non-equilibrium models. When geomorphologists discuss the form of rivers, for example, they emphasize initial conditions (bedrock) and cataclysmic events (superfloods) as determining the landscape. This was a shift away from the equilibrium approach that had dominated for several decades. In anthropology, the parallel to this approach was to look at history and individual agency—the ability of persons to act and effect change.

One of Rappaport's lasting contributions was his rejection of the prevailing view within the social sciences that the only function of religion was to bind the community through socially shared symbols. This century-old view was proposed by the French sociologist Émile Durkheim. Rappaport's study of the kaiko showed that rituals also had measurable material effects in ecosystems. They regulated such undeniably solid things as pig populations, the frequency of war, and the ratio of people to land. Some anthropologists disparaged such a utilitarian view of religion, but it also led to a new respect for the ability of traditional systems of knowledge to regulate environmental relationships. Rappaport disagreed with the notion that religion was no more than an illusion that was bound to disappear as reason and science advanced, and as it stands, religion has clearly persisted.

After his initial fieldwork with the Tsembaga Maring, Rappaport continued to use the concept of ecosystem in his work, but he came to be less interested in the flow of energy and matter in the food chain than he was in the flow of information. In considering an ecosystem as primarily a pathway for the flow of information, not of matter or energy, Rappaport was influenced by Gregory Bateson, another important ecological anthropologist.

Bateson had also done fieldwork in New Guinea, but 30 years before Rappaport. There he met Margaret Mead, later marrying and doing joint fieldwork with her in Bali. After New Guinea and Bali, Bateson contributed creatively to several disciplines, doing research on topics ranging from schizophrenia to dolphin communication. Both Bateson and Rappaport looked at ecosystems as self-organizing systems of information, drawing on cybernetics.

THE ECOSYSTEM CONCEPT IN ANTHROPOLOGY

So far, we have looked only at the concept of ecosystem within cultural anthropology. Eventually this concept became important in all the subfields of anthropology, especially biological anthropology and prehistoric archaeology.

Biological anthropologists adopted the ecosystem concept in the 1960s and 1970s through a set of interdisciplinary research projects called the International Biological Program. These projects studied human adaptation under extreme environmental conditions, including, among others, high mountains (the Andes) and Arctic cold (Alaska, Canada, and Greenland). They turned from the traditional physical anthropologist's measurements of human structure (height, weight, and shape) to studying function, such as the physiological adaptation to cold or oxygen deprivation.

Anthropologists constructed models of the flow of energy through these ecosystems. Among the people traditionally studied by anthropologists, most of the energy used by humans derived from food and firewood. Since the Industrial Revolution, energy from fossil fuels has become dominant, first in Europe and subsequently almost everywhere else. Even the Inuit of the far north now depend on petroleum, using snowmobiles and boat motors for transportation to their hunting and fishing grounds.

Like biological and cultural anthropologists, prehistoric archaeologists also adopted the ecosystem concept in the 1960s and continue to make substantial use of ecological approaches. They generally are not able to quantify energy flows because of the nature of their data, that is, primarily the trash and other artifacts of past societies. But they can study environmental variation over long time spans. These environmental changes are related to changes in human population and settlements, technology, and other features of material culture.

One of the most important things that students should take from their study of environmental anthropology is that humans are part of ecosystems, not separate from them. We are not simply managers of natural systems but are embedded in them. We are subject to limits and laws governing matter and energy, including the loss of energy with each step up the food chain (Cachelin, Norvell, and Darling 2010).

RECOMMENDED READING

Kendall M. Thu and E. Paul Durrenberger, eds. 1998. *Pigs, Profits, and Rural Communities*. Albany: State University of New York Press. Collection of essays introducing the problems related to industrial hog farming, primarily in Iowa.

Brad Weiss. 2016. *Real Pigs: Shifting Values in the Field of Local Pork*. Durham, NC: Duke University Press. Ethnography of raising pastured pigs in North Carolina provides entry into the local food movement and the resistance to global industrialized food production.

RECOMMENDED FILM

Adam Curtis, director. 2011. *All Watched Over by Machines of Loving Grace: Part 2. The Use and Abuse of Vegetational Concepts*. 60 minutes. BBC Productions. The development of the concept of the self-regulating ecosystem, in which cybernetic ideas are projected on to nature and human society.

Chapter Five

Amazonian Hunters

Beyond the tiny clearings populated by their thatched houses and manioc gardens, the Achuar occupy a vast area of tropical rain forest in the Upper Amazon. There are more than 5,000 Achuar people. Their territory lies in southeastern Ecuador and across the border in northern Peru. A French anthropologist, Philippe Descola, began living with the Achuar in 1976, working with his wife Anne-Christine Taylor, who is also an anthropologist. Many other anthropologists likewise began fieldwork among other Amazonian peoples, in a veritable explosion of new fieldwork, much of it addressing ecological questions. Rather than reducing these ethnographies of Amazonian farmer-hunters to a general picture, we will follow Descola as he describes an Achuar hunting trip (Descola 1994, 1996).

Pinchu, an Achuar hunter, set out at dawn, carrying his blowgun. He had dreamed about a drinking party at which he and his brother-in-law got drunk on manioc beer and quarreled violently. He considered this dream to be a good omen for encountering a herd of collared peccaries. Indeed, the previous afternoon, while gathering plants near the swamp, he had seen tracks of a herd of about 20 peccaries. Santamik, one of his two wives, came along to carry the food and baggage and, later, the meat. Were they not also accompanied by the nosy anthropologist, the hunting trip would have provided an opportunity for sex in privacy, away from the communal dwelling.

Santamik was also entirely responsible for the highly valued hunting dogs. Their care required more than simple feeding and training; the Achuar considered secret magical songs essential to the dogs' success in hunting. Ordinarily dogs would hunt armadillos and rodents such as agoutis and pacas. Only the most capable dogs were trusted to hunt dangerous peccaries or to tree an ocelot or jaguar. Dogs were not taken along to hunt arboreal animals (monkeys and birds) or when tracking and stalking game on the ground.

The Achuar method of hunting included the art of stalking: to approach silently, without startling the animal. Mastery of hunting required learning the behavior of the species that are hunted: imitating their calls, knowing their habitat, picking out and killing the dominant male, such as from a troop of howler monkeys, first, and predicting the response of a wounded animal. The blowgun was the main hunting weapon, propelling sharp, thin darts tipped with curare, a toxic mixture in which strychnine was the main poison. The Achuar believed that the potency of curare depended on members of the whole household obeying food taboos. Eating sweet foods, especially honey, was thought to weaken the hunter's lung power for using the blowgun, and eating salt might weaken the poison. The silence and accuracy of the Achuar blow-gun ensured that it was an efficient weapon, especially in dense forest. The blowgun had not been replaced by the shotgun for hunting game that lives high in the tree canopy, even though all Achuar men owned shotguns by the time of Descola's work, mostly for use in warfare.

In a typical day's hunting, a man would walk 30 to 45 kilometers, starting out on the main trail and switching to his barely visible hunting trails to explore an area of up to four square kilometers of steep, muddy, and thorny terrain. This was about a tenth of his hunting grounds.

AMAZONIAN GAME ANIMALS

Descola studied the take for 84 such hunting trips. These trips resulted in 106 kills, a total of 1,200 kilograms (about 2,600 pounds) of meat. Even though the Achuar name some 150 species of animals and birds that they regard as edible game, only 25 species were bagged in these 84 hunts. On this day, Pinchu first shot a woolly monkey, but it died wedged in a fork of the high tree, unrecoverable by the hunter. Later in the day Pinchu shot two collared peccaries. After butchering them, husband and wife each carried one home, ending an exhausting ten-hour day.

Of 25 species hunted, only a few species were obtained repeat-edly by Achuar hunters: white-lipped and collared peccaries, woolly monkeys, capuchin monkeys, agoutis, and two kinds of birds—toucans and curassows. The biggest kill was a tapir weighing 242 kilograms (532 pounds), but this animal is normally taboo, so including it in the total distorts the picture.

More than two-thirds of the remaining weight of meat was from two species of peccaries. Collared peccaries weigh about 20 kilograms (45 pounds) and travel in herds of up to ten individuals. White-lipped peccaries are larger—up to 30 kilograms (65 pounds). They travel in herds of 100 or more animals. Many of the other species of game mam-mals are difficult to hunt because they are small, arboreal, nocturnal, solitary, or rare. The peccaries, in contrast, are large, terrestrial, diur-nal, and abundant (though somewhat unpredictable in occurrence). Considering this, it is not surprising that peccaries are reported as the major game animal for many Amazonian societies.

Anthropologists who studied the Achuar claimed that hunting was organized in ways that enhanced its *sustainability*. Descola said that the knowledgeable Achuar hunter "takes care not to shoot wild sows that are pregnant or accompanied by young, in order to preserve the reproductive potential of a peccary horde" (Descola 1994:237). Another anthropologist who did fieldwork with the Achuar living across the border in Peru, Eric Ross (1978), pointed out that the Achuar avoided hunting many larger animals such as the tapir, capybara, sloth, and deer because of food taboos. Some of these taboos were mundane; others were based on the idea that these animals were reincarnated human spirits. Whatever the stated rationale, Ross argued that the species avoided were precisely those most vulnerable to overpredation. Other anthropologists resisted his conclusions, demanding data that would test his assertions about conservation more directly.

As studies of Amazon farmer-hunters progressed, many anthropologists were persuaded that the decisions the hunters make about what prey to pursue are most consistent with optimal foraging theory. Evolutionary ecologists developed this theory to describe nonhuman predator–prey relationships, but it seems also to apply for humans, at least in some societies. The theory suggests that hunters maximize their short-term rate of harvest even if this may threaten long-term stability by overhunting a vulnerable species.

An ethnography of Piro hunters in the Upper Amazon of Peru supports the *optimal foraging model*. The Piro hunted many of the same animals as the Achuar, but the Piro did not hunt with blowguns. Although proficient with bow and arrows, they used shotguns most of the time. During 18 months of fieldwork, Michael Alvard observed 79 Piro shotgun hunts directly and interviewed other hunters (Alvard 1995), finding that the collared peccary was by far the dominant game animal. The monkeys that the Piro most commonly shot were the spider monkey, howler monkey, and the capuchin.

Piro hunters did not altruistically limit their harvest of easily overhunted species such as tapir and monkeys. Nor did they avoid killing females or adult animals of prime age. Had they been consciously conserving the species, they would have concentrated on hunting mainly the young, the old, or the males of a species. In other words, the Piro were not behaving as "natural conservationists," trying to preserve biodiversity. Nonetheless, this does not mean that the Piro were behaving destructively. Because relatively small numbers of Indians were hunting over very large areas and using low technology, they did not have anywhere near the same destructive impact on game animals as today's loss of habitat to outsiders bulldozing the forest for logging, farming, and ranching.

Living adjacent to the Piro, but within Manu National Park, where shotgun hunting is not allowed, were Matsigenka communities whose hunters mostly used bows and arrows. A three-year study using trained indigenous monitors recorded more than 4,300 animals killed by 99 hunters. This was enough data to do computer simulations that led the authors to conclude that bow-and-arrow technology was adequate to provide for the hunters without endangering the survival of even vulnerable species such as spider monkeys (Shepard et al. 2012). The practical implication of their study was to suggest that it was not necessary to encourage the indigenous people to leave the park, as some environmentalists preferred. Rather they should be empowered to defend the parklands from loggers, ranchers, and gold miners. The researchers suggested that even with shotguns, Matsigenka outside the park would be compatible with conservation goals if they could be kept sedentary by attractions such as community schools and clinics and at the same time keep their more distant lands free of developers. These seemingly "unused" lands served as refuges for game animals to reproduce, maintaining the *resilience* of the system.

The resilience framework is the most recent approach for understanding hunter–prey populations in the Amazon. Rather than assuming game animal populations are reduced in a linear fashion as human population density increases, these studies show how prey populations bounce back. They can recover even in the face of shotgun hunting because hunters switch prey. For example, studies of the hunting in the relatively sedentary villages of Huaorani in the Ecuadorian Amazon in 1996–1997 and again five years later showed nearly double the biomass (in kg) of monkeys while the catch of the collared peccary, formerly the top prey animal, dropped to second, with only half the biomass in the earlier study (Lu 2010). Further, the refuge areas needed for the rebound of prey populations are no-man's lands traditionally maintained by warfare between Huaorani longhouses.

MANAGING THE FOREST

Historical ecologists point to clear signs that indigenous people have been managing the Amazonian forests for a long time. Extensive stands of palms with edible fruits, Brazil nut trees, bamboo, and other useful species that have been encouraged by humans are one such sign. Another kind of evidence is mounds, ditches, canals, causeways, and other significant earthworks. Tracts of fertile black soil (*terra preta*) mark the sites of old settlements and fields, enriched by ash, household debris, and organic mulch (Balée and Erickson 2006). These signs of an environment that was once more intensively managed are one of the clues to the devastating drop in human population throughout Amazonia after European contact. Beginning in the sixteenth century, Europeans introduced new diseases and violent exploitation.

Ironically, it was the post contact decimation of the indigenous population that made it possible for the Indians to do as much hunting as we have been describing. Estimates of the indigenous population of the Amazon vary widely, but we can judge that there were at least three times as many indigenous people in this area when the Europeans arrived as now, and perhaps very many more. Archaeologists exploring old village sites from the centuries just before European contact are finding many more large settlements with extensive earthworks. It would not have been possible to hunt successfully near such large established settlements (Roosevelt 1989).

Wanting to meet Amazonian people and see their forest environment for myself, I spent my summer vacation in 1972 visiting the Culina village of San Bernardo on the border of Peru and Brazil. I was accompanied by my husband, Bill, our almost two-year-old daughter, Alison, and Patsy Adams, a linguist/missionary/nurse. In this place where I was eating tapir liver, ceremonially drinking manioc beer, and rocking Alison to sleep in a locally woven hammock, one of my goals was to experience the differences between the New Guinea lowlands and Amazonia. As we flew low over the Amazon basin in a small plane, the endless green seemed tediously uniform, accustomed as we were to the more varied terrain of New Guinea from our earlier fieldwork. Underlying the apparent uniformity of all that green is an environmental complexity that anthropologists now appreciate more fully. Early studies made a simple two-way contrast between the *várzea*, the floodplain with soil enriched by sediments washed down from the Andes, and the *terra firme*, the high ground between rivers.

Anthropologists now find that this simple dichotomy needs to be disaggregated, that is, taken apart to make finer distinctions (Moran 1993). The várzea includes the Amazon estuary (affected by Atlantic tides), the lower floodplain with its wealth of fisheries, and the upper floodplain. In the terra firme we need to contrast several ecosystems, too. The lowland savanna has rather poor agricultural potential because of its acid soil and seasonally variable rainfall. Ecosystems in the watershed of blackwater rivers are the most difficult of all. These forests are so low in productivity that hunting is not very successful, and people depend more on fishing to supplement their bitter manioc harvest. Upland forests outside the floodplain of the Amazon and forests in the foothills of the Andes have soils that are more productive for agriculture. They are the greatest storehouse of the planet's biodiversity but also are the most threatened.

THE EVOLUTION OF
SOCIAL COMPLEXITY WITHIN AMAZONIA

Just as ecological anthropologists gradually came to understand in more detail the ecological differences within Amazonia, they also came to appreciate differences in political organization throughout the area. The Achuar, Piro, Matsigenka and Huaorani are egalitarian societies, lacking social stratification. Communities are small. When conflict arises in these societies, their communities tend to fission—part of the group moves away.

In past centuries, larger and more highly differentiated societies arose along the main river. These societies were led by paramount chiefs, political leaders with authority over more than just their small kinship group. These Amazonian chiefdoms collapsed soon after European contact, leaving behind archaeological evidence as well as the accounts of early European travelers (Roosevelt 1989). The rich resources of fish, turtles, and manatees provided the protein resources to sustain larger more sedentary villages well beyond anything that was possible among people of the areas between the main rivers, who relied more on hunting for protein.

In addition to fish, the riverine villages also had alluvial soils, enriched by the sediments from annual floods. These floods were also a hazard, especially for growing manioc, a root crop that requires more than a year to mature. The riverside farmers solved this problem by planting some of their fields on high ground, as insurance against the loss of crops in floods, and by planting quick-maturing maize. River transportation also facilitated long-distance trade.

As the population grew along the Amazon, people fought for the choice lands and village sites, as well as for other reasons. When the victors incorporated enemy groups that they had conquered, political groupings became more complex and hierarchical. In short, chiefdoms had evolved. One of the first anthropologists who articulated this ecological view of political development in Amazonia was Robert Carneiro. He also developed another theory of the origin of the state (Carneiro 1970). Like his view of the origin of chiefdoms in Amazonia, it emphasized ecological circumscription.

Where resources were concentrated in a limited area, warfare and competition over those resources led to conquest and internal stratification. In Amazonia, the riverine resources were somewhat *circumscribed*, but in the areas where the first states evolved, the Nile Valley and Mesopotamia, resources were extremely circumscribed. In these areas, narrow fertile valleys ran through deserts where agriculture was impossible without irrigation, and the states that emerged had social inequality and centralized government, as did chiefdoms; the central government in a state, however, is territorially based and has much more power than a chief. A state has the power to collect taxes, draft soldiers or workers, and use violence to enforce laws. The next chapter will introduce some anthropologists who have used ecological approaches in studying state societies.

RECOMMENDED READING

Glenn H. Shepard, an ethnobotanist, anthropologist, and filmmaker blogs from
Brazil at *Notes from the Ethnoground*, http://ethnoground.blogspot.com.br/
?m=1. Many other anthropologists and anthropological organizations have
blogs that are listed at http://www.livinganthropologically.com. One long-
running collective blog, *Savage Minds*, occasionally has posts on environmental anthropology, such as a 2017 series on Andean climate change. This
blog is now renamed *Anthrodendum*, https://savageminds.org

RECOMMENDED FILM

Joe Beringer, director/producer. 2009. *Crude.* 100 minutes. Radical Media. Follows part of the class action lawsuit for environmental damages brought
against Chevron by Ecuadorians living in the Amazonian rain forest.
Adrian Cowell, director. 1987. *Banking on Disaster.* 78 minutes. Bullfrog
Films. A condensation of Cowell's series *The Decade of Destruction* documenting the peak period of the destruction of the Amazonian forest in the
1980s. Shows the serious consequences of building a World Bank-funded
road through the Brazilian rain forest.
Adrian Cowell, director. 2002. *The Fires of the Amazon.* 44 minutes. Bullfrog
Films. Updates the situation in the Amazon, where the destruction of forest continued, despite some gains in environmental protection.

Chapter Six

Complex Societies

U ntil now this book has been concerned mostly with hunters and gatherers and tropical forest farmers. These societies are small in scale. A local group of seed gatherers in the Great Basin of western North America typically did not exceed a few families, a total of 25 persons. In New Guinea the local population of Tsembaga Maring was about 200 people, a size typical of tropical forest farmers. Each settlement was self-sufficient economically, except for a few significant items obtained in trade. Several settlements might be grouped into a political unit or alliance of a few thousand people at most.

Studying small populations no larger than those of the Amazon or New Guinea seemed a necessity for ecological anthropologists who hoped to measure the flow of energy and materials through an ecosystem. When ecological anthropologists turned to fieldwork in rural communities that were part of large nations, some of them decided to analyze those communities as ecosystems. They took the relatively small community in which they did their fieldwork as the unit of study. For example, Brooke Thomas was one of the anthropologists associated with the Man in the Andes project of the International Biological Program (Thomas 1976). The project leaders chose the district of Nuñoa in Peru as its unit of study. The district appeared to be isolated both geographically and socially. Mountain ranges surrounded it on three sides, and most of the 7,750 inhabitants were Quechua Indians with little involvement in Peruvian national culture. Taking an even smaller unit of study, Thomas presented much of his data for a typical family of six, consisting of parents with four children 2 to 17 years of age.

The people of Nuñoa cultivate potatoes and the grains quinoa and cañihua, traditional Andean crops well adapted to the climate. They herd alpaca, sheep, and llama, animals that can cope with the short pasture grasses that grow at high altitude. As a human biologist who was also an ecological anthropologist, Thomas was interested in the flow of energy through the ecosystem. All the energy that flowed through the Nuñoan family had its origin from the sun, taken up directly into their crops and herds. They were not using forms of stored solar energy such as gas and oil or electricity from hydroelectric or nuclear power. The family consumed energy in the form of meat, cereals, and potatoes from their own harvest. This can be measured or estimated as calories. They also expended energy in farming, herding, and other activities that Thomas measured or estimated. He could even estimate the amount of animal dung they needed to collect from their corral for use as fertilizer and fuel.

At the end of all Thomas's measurements and calculations of energy flow through this Andean family, the striking fact was that they were not as isolated as they might initially have appeared. Only about one-quarter of the food consumed by the family came from their own fields and herds. The other three-quarters consisted of foods that they purchased, such as wheat flour, maize, sugar, and alcohol made from sugarcane. All these high-energy items came from lower altitudes. To obtain them, the Nuñoans marketed wool, hides, and meat.

Few Nuñoan families owned land; they were therefore obliged to do farming and herding work at least 40 days a year for wealthy owners of large estates, the *haciendas*. In the years following Thomas's study, increasing dependence on the market and wage labor made it inappropriate to consider the household or the district as an isolated unit. Thomas himself was no longer satisfied with the simplifying assumptions that he had made for his energy flow analysis. He recognized the significance of social inequalities and economic change (Thomas 1997). To cope with this, ecological anthropologists needed to find new ways to deal with larger units in complex societies. What is more, it was clear that even small indigenous societies were historically subject to powerful forces from the states and empires within which they existed, even if travelers might want to depict them as exotic and pristine.

THE ECOLOGY OF STATES

Beginning with Julian Steward, who turned his attention from the Great Basin to the Caribbean region, other ecological anthropologists did their fieldwork in larger populations of thousands or millions. Large societies are politically organized as states rather than bands, tribes, or chiefdoms. They depend on intensive agriculture, planting grain in terraced or irrigated fields. They consciously reshape their environments to a far greater degree than small societies like the Maring or the Achuar.

Although many anthropologists working in complex societies took small rural communities within them as their units of study, others broke out of this mold. The Norwegian anthropologist Fredrik Barth, for example, focused on larger units. About 500,000 people lived in Swat State in Pakistan when Barth did his fieldwork there. They comprised three major ethnic groups speaking unrelated languages. By far the largest group was the Pathans, sedentary agriculturalists. They raised wheat, maize, and rice in irrigated fields in the broad fertile valleys of the Indus and Swat Rivers. In his classic paper, "Ecologic Relationships of Ethnic Groups in Swat, North Pakistan," Barth (1956, 2007), introduced the concept of the *ecological niche* from biology into anthropology.

Occupying another niche, the Kohistanis were a smaller group. They probably controlled the area from ancient times before being invaded by the Pathans and retreating into their more marginal lands at higher altitudes. The steep terrain required that they construct terraces for their narrow fields of maize and millet. At these higher altitudes, the summer is short, yielding only one crop of grain each year rather than the two crops at lower altitudes.

The third ethnic group in Swat State was the Gujars. Many of them were true nomadic herders with only sheep and goats, obtaining their grain from the Pathans. They can be thought of as a herding caste in the Pathan caste hierarchy. (In *caste* systems, people inherit their social position and occupation.) Other Gujars were less fully committed to nomadism. The wives were left to tend the fields and buffaloes every summer while the men took the sheep and goats to pastures in the high mountains.

In Barth's terms, each of these three ethnic groups occupied a different ecological niche. This is a slightly different use of the term than in biology. In biology, different niches are occupied by different species, whereas Barth applied it to different ethnic groups of the same species, *Homo sapiens*.

INDONESIAN AGRICULTURE

Just as Barth is known for introducing the term *ecological niche* into anthropology, Clifford Geertz is noted for introducing the term *ecosystem*. Geertz described "swidden" and "sawah" as two agricultural ecosystems in Indonesia, the fourth most populous country in the world (Geertz 1963).

Sawah (an Indonesian word) is the ecosystem of the flooded paddy rice field. Within Indonesia, sawah is found primarily in densely populated Java and Bali. The irrigation water does more than simply water the rice plants. It brings nutrients to the fields from volcanic rock at the headwaters. It regulates oxygen and pH of the soil as well as controlling soil microbes and crop pests of all kinds. The water needs to be kept gently flowing rather than stagnant. Timing is crucial, as the fields need to be drained for planting, weeding, and harvesting, with the water level allowed to rise gradually as the rice plants grow. All of this requires maintaining an elaborate system of canals, ditches, and terraced fields, a complete reworking of the natural landscape. Recent archaeological investigations on Bali indicate that even the most ancient of these irrigation structures are constantly under renegotiation and reconstruction (Lansing et al. 2006).

Swidden, now more commonly called slash-and-burn *horticulture*, is found in the Outer Islands of Indonesia, the less populated islands stretching from Sumatra to New Guinea. Geertz described the swidden plot as a "canny imitation" of the tropical forest. Like the tropical forest it replaces, the field has a high degree of diversity, with many interplanted crop varieties. Like the tropical forest, the swidden grows on infertile soils, its nutrients largely locked up in the living plants. The cutting and burning that precede planting are a way of not simply clearing the land but also making the minerals in the ash readily available for the new crop.

Geertz's influential book *Agricultural Involution* (1963) is mostly devoted to analyzing Indonesia's colonial history and its implications for agriculture. The production of export crops was particularly significant: sugar in Java, and rubber, coconuts, coffee, and other tree crops in the Outer Islands. The pressure of population growth was great on the intensively used lands of Java.

In the decade after Geertz's work, the Green Revolution came to Indonesian agriculture. Indonesia's government adopted an agricultural policy that was intended to increase rice production by introducing the newly developed varieties of rice. In the 1970s the government invested its oil revenues in extending credit to farmers so that they could purchase the fertilizers and pesticides that were required by the new hybrid rice. To get two or even three crops per year, the government urged farmers to replant the rice fields as quickly after harvest as possible. They abandoned the planting and irrigation schedules traditionally organized by the water temples.

Bali's temples are devoted to a hierarchy of gods and goddesses that ranges from major Hindu gods down to local deities. Their shrines are associated with lakes, springs, and canals. The Balinese call their religion *Agama Tirtha*, the religion of holy water. Sprinkled on or imbibed by worshippers, the holy water is both a blessing—as it comes from upstream—and a purification—as it flows downstream, carrying away impurity.

The congregation of each Balinese water temple consists of people who live and farm in that watershed. For much of the year the temple stands empty, but at least twice a year people gather for festivals and offerings. They also meet to make decisions about what to plant and when to release irrigation water. The decisions they make ensure that the water is distributed fairly and that crop rotation between rice, vegetables, and fallow periods will help to control pests.

Working with a systems ecologist, the anthropologist Stephen Lansing concluded from computer simulations that hundreds of local farmer associations, each managing a small part of the system of rice terraces and dams, find their way to decisions that are close to optimal for the entire system. Downstream farmers are more concerned about water shortages and argue for staggered plantings, to make sure water will be available when they need it. Upstream farmers are more worried about pests and press for coordinated planting. Pest damage is greater if plantings are staggered, and pests such as insects and rats can move from one field to the next (Lansing 2006; Lansing and de Vet 2012).

The new agricultural policy of quickly replanting the rice fields turned sour when a series of pests devastated the crops. The hybrid varieties proved susceptible to disease, and the new irrigation gates and fertilizers were damaging to the ecology of the rice terraces. Discouraged farmers on Bali, the Indonesian island east of Java, asked to have the control of irrigation and planting turned back over to the priests of the water temples.

Foreign agricultural consultants were skeptical of the idea that religion could have anything to do with pest control. Nor did the anthropologist who set out as a graduate student in the 1970s to study the cultural history of Balinese temples, Stephen Lansing, expect to wind up studying agricultural pests. Lansing may not have designed his research with the intention of testing Roy Rappaport's theory that ritual regulates environmental relationships—Rappaport's work was not cited in Lansing's book. Yet, it would be hard to imagine a more convincing demonstration of Rappaport's point than these Balinese temples and the rituals associated with them.

VILLAGES IN THE ALPS

The Alps hold a special place in the history of ecological anthropology because two important anthropologists did fieldwork in Alpine villages that helped to move ecological anthropology in a new direction. Each of these anthropologists turned to Europe after he had become well established by major research done elsewhere: Eric Wolf did his earlier work in Latin America, and Robert Netting did his in West Africa. In turning to Europe, both Wolf and Netting chose to work in small rural communities. Anthropologists were slow to get into the study of urban ecology.

The village of Törbel is perched high in the Swiss Alps. Villagers support themselves by raising dairy cattle, sheep, and goats in mountain pastures, planting rye and other grains for bread, and gathering wood for housing and heat. There were 125 households in Törbel during Netting's 1970–1971 fieldwork. To describe this village in Switzerland Netting borrowed a concept that Eric Wolf had developed in peasant villages of Latin America, that of the closed corporate community. *Closed* in this case is quite literal. In 300 years of parish records only three men had settled in Törbel from outside to marry and raise a family, though many had migrated out.

Balancing on an Alp is the revealing title that Netting (1981) gave to his study—"balancing" or stability was very much the theme of the work. Over the centuries, the village "changed only enough not to have to change." Relatively high mortality, late marriage, and frequent celibacy restrained population growth. When gradual population growth did begin to put pressure on food resources in the late nineteenth century, Törbel farmers added potatoes as a new staple food to get higher yields than they had with grain alone.

Netting continued to call what he was doing "cultural ecology," in the tradition of Steward. His work shared an interest in equilibrium in ecosystems with the newer ecological anthropology of Rappaport and others. What was new was his addition of the historical dimension. This was made possible by 300 years of parish records of births, deaths, and marriages. The oldest documents in Törbel's archives recorded land sales as far back as the thirteenth century.

For his Alpine fieldwork, Eric Wolf chose the German-speaking village of St. Felix and the Romance-language-speaking village of Tret in the Tyrol region of northern Italy. Wolf was familiar with the Tyrol, having vacationed there with his family as a boy, later returning when he served with the U.S. mountain troops at the end of World War II. The whole area was part of the Austro-Hungarian Empire until World War I, when it was incorporated into Italy. The villages are only a half hour's walk apart, but they have different ethnic identities. People from the two groups distrusted each other and held negative stereotypes of each other as overly orderly versus disorderly, stingy versus spendthrift, and so on.

Wolf did fieldwork in the two villages in 1960–1962, work that was followed up by his student John W. Cole in 1965–1967 (Cole and Wolf 1974). Their joint research concentrated on inheritance, one of the major cultural differences between the two otherwise very similar villages. The German speakers of St. Felix asserted that the eldest son inherited the land. The residents of Tret favored division of the inheritance. As their study progressed, Wolf and Cole discovered that there was more similarity in the actual practice of inheritance and ecological adaptation than in the contrasting ideas about social structure that people expressed. The researchers concluded that the very real differences in outlook and family structure were not due to microenvironmental differences, as they had initially hypothesized, but to their historical links to larger cultural entities: the Germanic empire to the north and Mediterranean to the south.

Writing about the Alps, Eric Wolf (1972) proposed to use the term *political ecology* to understand cultural adaptation by considering other societies as part of the environment, as well as features of the biophysical environment such as climate and terrain. As you will see throughout this text, it is rarely possible to understand fully the relationship between a population of humans and some other species without getting into questions of power and inequality. That seems to be true whether the other species are trees in a rain forest, microorganisms that cause disease, or fish threatened by industrial pollution of a river. By the 1980s and 1990s, political ecology came to be the most widely used approach in environmental anthropology (Biersack and Greenberg 2006; Paulson and Gezon 2005).

Chapter 7 will look at an extended example of political ecology based on the inequality of power and wealth between transnational corporations, the government of a small island-nation, and small populations of tropical forest villagers. The mining of nonrenewable resources—copper and gold ore—devastated the river basin from which the people living downstream from the mine derived their subsistence.

INDUSTRIAL FARMING

The rural communities mentioned so far in this chapter were supported by small farms, with the partial exception of the Andean haciendas mentioned in the first example. Around the world, land controlled by small farmers is increasingly disappearing before an onslaught of large-scale industrial farming. I returned home to a high-school class reunion not long ago to find the small mixed-crop farm on which I grew up newly merged with its neighbors into massive monocropped cornfields as the drought-stricken Corn Belt expanded into the better-watered land of southwestern Michigan.

Industrial agriculture as currently practiced is not sustainable because it degrades the soil through erosion by wind and water, through chemical processes such as salinization from the intrusion of sea water and the evaporation of irrigation water, and through physical processes such as compaction. Water drawn for irrigation is depleting *fossil aquifers*, notably the Ogallala Aquifer under the Great Plains of the United States and the deep aquifer under the North China Plain. Industrial agriculture makes a major contribution to climate change while it is also under pressure from the variable effects of global climate change.

The trend to industrial agriculture has swallowed up small farms in many countries as land is sold or leased to create large monocrop plantations of crops for export. Some of the growing demand is for crops that can be used for biofuels—corn, sugar, and oil palm (Li 2014:180). Often the purchasers are transnational agribusiness corporations. Efficiencies of scale allow them to afford large farm machinery

that replaces much of the labor formerly required. Though some former landowners may find work, others will have to migrate to cities.
Heavy use of fossil-carbon-based fuels, fertilizers, and pesticides,
genetically modified crops, and concentrated animal feeding operations (CAFOs) replaced older farming methods. These developments,
as well as local resistance to them, form the background to current
work by anthropologists.

RECOMMENDED READING

James B. Greenberg and Thomas K. Park. 1994. "Political Ecology." *Journal of
    Political Ecology* 1(1):1–13. Their editorial note on the founding of this
    open-access journal remains the best definition of this paradigm for study.
Kendall Thu. 2010. "CAFOs Are in Everyone's Backyard: Industrial Agricul-
    ture, Democracy, and the Future." In *CAFO: The Tragedy of Industrial
    Animal Factories*, ed. Daniel Imhoff. cafothebook.org. The CAFO industry
    has insulated itself from government regulation and suppressed scientific
    research to a dangerous extent, Thu argues.
UNESCO. *Maya Site of Copan*. Multimedia introduction to the World Heritage
    Site in Honduras. http://whc.unesco.org/en/list/129/

RECOMMENDED FILM

J. Stephen Lansing and Andre Singer. 1988. *The Goddess and the Computer*.
    58 minutes. Documentary Educational Resources. Lansing shows the
    resource management practices of the priests of Balinese water temples
    and the development of a computer model that demonstrated the effec-
    tiveness of the system.

Chapter Seven

The Underground Environment
Minerals

Copper was the first metal to be used by humans. This is because native copper (that is, copper in nearly pure metallic form) occurs in pieces that are large enough to be useful much more commonly than native iron, gold, or silver. Deposits of native copper were found in northern Michigan and made into tools and ornaments by Native Americans 3,000 years ago, long before Europeans arrived. Native copper had been used in the Middle East even earlier. By 10,000 years ago, people hammered and rolled native copper into awls, hooks, beads, and pendants. These early metalworkers experimented with heating copper ore in a charcoal fire and soon developed the process of smelting—extracting metallic copper from copper in mineral form. The simple processes they used required very high-grade ores—oxides and sulfides containing more than 50 percent metal. Only in the past century has technology been developed that allows miners to exploit large deposits of low-grade ore, that is, rock containing less than 1 percent metal.

At the beginning of the twentieth century, steam shovels dug the first open-pit copper mine at Bingham Canyon in Utah. Nowadays open-pit mines use diesel- and electric-powered equipment. Mining has a massive impact on the physical landscape. The mining and quarrying industries move over 57 billion tons of earth each year, exceeding the amount of earth moved by natural physical processes; water erosion moves an estimated 53 billion tons of earth each year (Bridge 2004).

The ability to use low-grade ores means that for every ton of usable metal extracted, more than a hundred tons of finely ground rock particles are discarded from the mine's process plant as tailings. The overburden—the dirt and rock that was moved to uncover the ore—adds to the waste eroding into streams and rivers. For many years, these wastes were simply dumped around the mines. Sometimes the risk of lawsuits from farmers downstream led mining companies to retain the wastes behind tailings dams until eventually many governments passed environmental laws prohibiting the discharge of mine wastes into rivers. Less-industrialized countries were often too desperate for economic growth to pass or enforce environmental laws that might discourage foreign investors from developing the mining industry.

THE OK TEDI MINE, PAPUA NEW GUINEA

One of the largest open-pit copper mines in the world is the Ok Tedi Mine in the Star Mountains of Papua New Guinea (PNG). Between 1987 and 2016 the mine shipped a total of 16.8 million metric tons of ore concentrate to overseas smelters where it was processed to produce 4.6 million metric tons of copper, 12.6 million ounces of gold, and 30.2 million ounces of silver (OTML 2017). To accomplish this, miners needed to dig up and move at least 60 billion metric tons of ore and waste rock each year. The amount of copper contained in ore is about one half of one percent, and the percent of gold is tiny, less than one part in a million. When I visited there in 1983, the mine was still under construction. It had not yet begun to produce copper, but some of its impact on the environment was already visible. Rain forest had been bulldozed to construct the process plant, town site, roads, air-strips, and other facilities. Erosion made once-clear streams run muddy into the Ok Tedi, the river for which the mine is named.

The Ok Tedi is a tributary of the Fly River, one of the great rivers of the tropics. Because of the heavy rainfall in its headwaters, the Fly is noted for having the highest runoff per unit area of any river in the world. As we motored in a dugout canoe on the Middle Fly with villagers going to their gardens to pick bananas, it was hard to imagine that the mine would eventually have a significant impact here, more than 300 miles (nearly 500 km) downstream.

The Fly River flows through an area that was once linked to northern Australia by a narrow land bridge that has since disappeared. Thousands of Australian birds—tall egrets, glossy ibis, and magpie geese—spend the dry season in the Fly region. The birds, like the village fisherfolk, depend on the unique fish fauna of the Fly.

Developing the Ok Tedi mine required that more than one large transnational company be involved. The major investor in Ok Tedi was the largest Australian mining company, Broken Hill Proprietary (BHP). The American oil company Amoco was trying to diversify into mining in the 1980s and joined BHP in this venture. A group of German companies also invested, trying to ensure a steady supply of copper concentrate for their smelters. The Papua New Guinea government also became a partner. These investors built a road and pipeline between the mine and the Fly River port at Kiunga from which copper concentrate would be shipped downriver by barge and loaded on ocean-going ships for smelting in Asia, Australia, and Germany.

Beginning in 1984, mining transformed Mount Fubilan from a 2,094 m (6,880-foot) mountain to a big hole in the ground. Fubilan had special significance to the indigenous people as marking the underground land of the dead and the mythological source of *fubi*, one type of stone axe. Having obtained steel axes in recent years, they no longer needed to trade for stone axes, but they still deemed Fubilan a sacred place, connected by underground passages to other sacred sites and mines. The indigenous mythology of this region is a living tradition that continues to evolve, incorporating ideas derived from contemporary politics and evangelical Christianity (Jorgensen 2014; Macdonald 2017).

To the mining company, Fubilan was a geological prize because its gold-rich cap could be exploited first, giving the quick financial return needed to build additional facilities to process the lower-grade copper ore beneath. One of those facilities was a dam intended to retain the mine wastes that would otherwise enter the river system. The agreements had assumed that a tailings dam would be constructed, limiting environmental damage to the upper Ok Tedi. After numerous delays and under pressure, the Papua New Guinea government agreed to proceed without a dam, continuing to allow mine wastes to enter the river system.

IMPACT OF THE MINE ON THE LANDOWNERS

Most of the land required for the Ok Tedi mine was owned by the Wopkaimin, an ethnic group of some 700 people (documented in the 1980 Census). In 1973 an ecological anthropologist, David Hyndman, began fieldwork with the Wopkaimin (Hyndman 1994). He was especially interested in hunting, the passion of Wopkaimin men. With bows and arrows, they ranged the rain forests from altitudes of 1,500 feet (457 m) above sea level at the banks of the Ok Tedi to a high plateau at 8,000 feet (2,458 m). Hyndman found that four prey species accounted for most of Wopkaimin hunting success. The most frequently taken game animals were two small tree-living marsupials—the silky cuscus and the coppery ringtail. The largest game animals were *feral* pigs and cassowaries.

Hyndman observed that both men and women worked in gardens, growing many crops, of which the staple, taro, contributed two-thirds of the calories in the diet. They planted groves of palm trees for food, including fruit and nut pandanus and starchy sago palms. The women raised pigs. They collected and ate fish, frogs, wild greens, and ferns, contributing to a diverse diet in the years prior to the opening of the mine.

The opening of the mine altered Wopkaimin life drastically, as Hyndman discovered when he returned in the 1980s. Abandoning their rain forest hamlets, the Wopkaimin had crowded into roadside villages. During the construction of the mine between 1982 and 1984, over half of Wopkaimin men worked as unskilled wage laborers, eating in the company dining halls and buying tinned meat and fish for their families to replace the game they no longer hunted. Wives continued to garden, raising sweet potatoes to replace the more demanding taro crop. Beer was one of the few items available for purchase with the men's wages. Drinking led to fights, adultery, and rape. Cash income, though not large by Euro-American standards, transformed the subsistence economy and ripped the social fabric.

In the new roadside villages, health changes took place. Malaria increased with the shift of residence to lower altitudes. Sexually transmitted diseases increased, along with prostitution. In time, as the company opened the health services it had developed for employees to the community at large, there was improvement in community health near the mine, though not more widely in the province.

DOWNSTREAM IMPACT OF THE OK TEDI MINE

The social impact of the mine was undoubtedly greatest among the people who lived closest to the mine. The Wopkaimin lost about 10 percent of their rain forest to the mine. However, a more significant environmental impact was yet to come to villages downstream that had not received any income from leasing their land or being employed in construction. The first big sign of trouble, in June of 1984, was a spill of cyanide, the chemical used in extracting gold at the Ok Tedi Mine. Dead fish and crocodiles came floating down the Ok Tedi.

By 1987, a less toxic but more substantial discharge was having observable environmental impact. Mine tailings and waste rock were overflowing the banks and building up in the lower reaches of the Ok Tedi, destroying trees and gardens as finely ground tailings smothered the land. Monitoring of fish populations by the mining company scientists confirmed that the Ok Tedi was biologically dead. Copper in the river water decimated the invertebrates on which fish fed, and flooding damaged important riverside habitats. New and dangerous river currents made it difficult to navigate by canoe. These problems would increase in extent and move down the Fly River, if mining continued in this manner. Recovery time would be measured in centuries rather than years. None of this was anticipated in the environmental impact studies published before mining began, which had been done with the assumption that the wastes would be properly handled (Townsend and Townsend 2003).

Stuart Kirsch, the anthropologist who did research in the villages of the lower Ok Tedi, was not an ecological anthropologist and had not intended to study the Yonggom subsistence system as Hyndman had studied Wopkaimin hunting. Kirsch was a cultural anthropologist studying the Yonggom symbolic world, particularly their magic and sorcery. Soon Yonggom distress at the environmental damage thrust Kirsch into a different role than he had planned, that of acting as an advocate and mediator. His research shifted focus from the village to the global system. The villagers themselves became environmental activists, taking their story to corporate shareholder meetings, the International Water Tribunal, the German press, and the United Nations "Earth Summit" in Rio de Janeiro (Kirsch 2006, 2014).

In May 1994, the Yonggom and other downstream villagers took their case to court in Melbourne, Australia, the corporate headquarters of BHP. The civil suit was settled out of court two years later. Along with monetary compensation, the downstream villagers had extracted a promise that the mining company would build a dam or other means of retaining the mine tailings and other mine waste. In 1998, the mining company hired a company to begin dredging sand from the lower Ok Tedi and storing it adjacent to the river. Dredging will probably continue as long as mining continues. It removes enough volume of waste to reduce, but not eliminate, the problem of overbank flooding and to keep the Fly River navigable by the company barges. New problems are postponed, at least until someday the river may change its course and eat away the storage areas. In 2000, the villagers filed another lawsuit, charging BHP with breach of contract for failing to resolve the tailings problem. With the permission of the Papua New Guinea Parliament in 2001, BHP Billiton left, transferring its majority share of ownership in the mine to a trust that BHP established in Singapore. The trust would invest profits from the continued operation of the mine on behalf of the downstream communities and their heirs. In return, BHP was given questionable indemnity from future claims for environmental damage.

Another environmental problem soon became obvious to all along the levees of the Middle Fly River—acid mine drainage formed when sulfides in the tailings reacted with oxygen. In 2013, the Papua New Guinea Government nationalized the mine. After the departure of all the transnational corporations, even those Papua New Guineans downstream of the mine suffering the most negative environmental impact tended to favor continued operation of the mine. They held out little hope of redress if mining were to cease. Unfortunately, the deeper ore contains even more of the acid-producing sulfur, although in 2009 the mine management began treating tailings to remove part of it. Acid mine drainage from sulfides already in the flood plain will continue long after mine closure and may render riverside villages uninhabitable.

In 2015, residents got a taste of the impact that permanent closure of the mine will eventually bring to this region. In El Niño years, drought hits the Fly and Ok Tedi, while La Niña years bring flooding. The dry season of both 1997–1998 and 2015–2016 brought especially strong droughts. The mine's management closed the mine for eight months during the 2015–2016 drought, citing the difficulty of shipping out copper ore and bringing in diesel fuel by barge at low water levels. The abrupt layoffs sent PNG workers back to home villages that were suffering food shortages because of the drought. Expatriate workers were also sent home, allowing management to institute major cost-cutting changes in the labor force at a time when metal prices were already low and to increase the profit margin after reopening. The spin-off from the closure had dramatic effects. The mining town was suddenly a ghost town, with its school and hospital closed as well as many of the businesses that had sprung up to serve the mine (Jorgensen 2016; Macdonald 2017).

INDIGENOUS PEOPLE AND ENVIRONMENTAL HUMAN RIGHTS

The failure to build a tailings dam at Ok Tedi showed a reckless disregard for the environment that would not be permitted in the home countries of the investing companies—Australia, Germany, Canada, and the United States. Yet Ok Tedi is by no means the most serious environmental offender among mines. On the same island, but across the border to the west of Ok Tedi, in the Indonesian province of West Papua, the American company Freeport-McMoRan developed the much larger Ertsberg-Grasberg copper-gold mine. Unlike their relatives in Papua New Guinea, the indigenous people of West Papua were not even recognized as owners of the land or compensated for environmental damage from mining. Many local people in the heavily militarized mining area were killed by Indonesian troops.

In such cases where human rights are violated, anthropologists often serve as advocates for the rights of the people they have studied. Sometimes they bring their concerns to a wider group of anthropologists, such as the American Anthropological Association (AAA). The AAA has a permanent, elected committee working on issues of human rights. They may also enlist the aid of nongovernment human rights organizations.

Many of the violations of basic human rights of indigenous people have a basis in conflict over natural resources. Historically, ethnic minorities were pushed into areas unsuitable for farming and industry. The discovery of oil or minerals and the need for timber in the industrialized world abruptly removed the protection their isolation once afforded them. Indigenous people who live at great distances from the centers of power and wealth have something in common with the most impoverished people in industrial societies. Both groups are asked to bear a disproportionate share of the risk associated with industry while receiving a smaller share of its benefits.

RECOMMENDED READING

Environmental Justice Atlas, an interactive map based on a database of environmental conflicts, including the mines at Ok Tedi and Freeport, http://ejatlas.org. The atlas was produced by an international project whose main website contains other resources including videos: http://www.ejolt.org/section/resources/videos/. It is coordinated from the environmental institute at the Universitat Autònoma de Barcelona (UAB).

Jerry K. Jacka. 2015. *Alchemy in the Rain Forest: Politics, Ecology, and Resilience in a New Guinea Mining Area*. Durham, NC: Duke University Press. Ethnography in a Papua New Guinea Highlands society illustrates new perspectives in ecological anthropology two generations after Rappaport as well as the inequality and violence too often engendered by mining projects.

RECOMMENDED FILMS

Christopher McCleod, director. 2013. "Profit and Loss." 55 minutes. Part of the series *Standing on Sacred Ground*. Earth Island Institute/Bullfrog Films. Papua New Guineans displaced by the Ramu nickel mine and Canadian First Nations damaged by the Tar Sands oil industry speak out.

Numerous short clips of the Ok Tedi Mine from EMTV, Papua New Guinea's television station, are available on YouTube.

Chapter Eight

Warfare Ecology

Anthropologists define warfare to include organized, deadly combat between communities, whether relatively small political units, such as villages of a few hundred hunter-horticulturalists, or nation-states of millions. The technology of warfare is similarly variable, ranging from bows and arrows to nuclear bombs. We referred to small-scale warfare within noncentralized societies in earlier chapters. In this chapter, our concern is with global wars and contemporary insurgencies and their impact on environments.

It is rarely possible to measure ecological damage from warfare scientifically. The one case where scientific surveys documented both prewar and postwar conditions and unpolluted control sites is the Persian Gulf War of 1991 (Brauer 2009:81–117). Unlike later wars in this region, this one was short, lasting from August 9, 1990, when Iraqi troops invaded Kuwait, until the March 3, 1991, cease-fire. When Allied air forces entered the war on January 16, 1991, Iraqi troops set fire to Kuwait's oil wells and released oil from storage tanks. The resulting air and water pollution had a dramatic but relatively brief effect on living things, because air and water circulate quickly; damage to land, especially desert land, lasts longer.

Ecology, engineering, and other disciplines use the term *warfare ecology* to refer to the environmental impact of war. Not limited to the active phase of hostilities, it includes the manufacture and testing of weapons and the environmental aftermath of war. Even during peacetime, the standing militaries of industrialized nations are massive consumers of fossil energy, contributing to the greenhouse gases causing climate chaos.

Unexploded bombs, depleted uranium, and land mines may alter the environment for many years. Ethnographer Eleana Kim describes the border between North and South Korea, the ironically named Demilitarized Zone (DMZ), as "the most heavily militarized border in the world, with more than a million soldiers on each side and a million land mines within it" (Kim 2014:65). U.S. and UN forces laid these land mines during the Korean War that ended in 1953. Later, during the Cold War, both North and South Koreans laid more.

Land mines may lie in wait for a long time. Designed to be triggered by humans, they may also be set off by a wild boar or deer but not by lighter-weight animals. Hence, the unpopulated border strip of the DMZ, 250 km long and 4 km wide, and the adjacent area, the Civilian Control Zone (CCZ), has become somewhat of a refuge for birds and other species, including 106 rare and endangered species. This has led to the adjacent area being promoted as the "Peace and Life Zone" and even an ecotourism destination, symbolized by the migration of flights of cranes, including the rare red-crowned crane, which breeds in summer in northeastern Russia and overwinters in the DMZ (Kim 2016).

SMALL WARS: LARGE DAMAGE

Around the world on any day, in dozens of small-scale insurgencies and civil wars, combatants use small arms such as assault rifles, improvised explosive devices (IEDs), machetes, and the like. This is not to say that large nation-states are not involved; they may supply firearms, intervene on one side or the other, or provide financial support by purchasing minerals or drugs from war zones. Small internal wars can produce large environmental damage, particularly by creating streams of desperate displaced persons (Brauer 2009:158). The damage commonly includes deforestation in search of firewood, poaching of large mammals, and illegal mining.

When internal conflict drags on for many years, the environmental damage mounts up. Protracted conflict in central Africa has drawn special attention from anthropologists and conservationists because of its implications for threatened species of primates. The Virunga Volcanoes area is a mountainous area up to 3,500 meters altitude (11,500 feet) that spans the borders of Rwanda, Uganda, and the Democratic Republic of Congo (DRC, formerly called Zaire). Much of this forested area is formally part of protected areas: the Mghinga Gorilla National Park in Uganda, the Volcanoes National Park in Rwanda, and the largest, the Virunga National Park in eastern DRC. Primatologist Dian Fossey established the Karisoke Research Station in Volcanoes National Park in 1967 as a field base to study the mountain gorilla (*Gorilla gorilla beringei*), which was classified as Critically Endangered. The population of mountain gorillas had dropped below 300, but thanks to intensive conservation efforts (at the cost of lives of park rangers killed by poachers) it rose to 880 by 2016.

Another subspecies, Grauer's gorilla (*Gorilla beringei graueri*), in its stronghold of Kahuzi-Biega National Park in eastern DRC, was not as well-known or studied as the mountain gorilla. It had been classified as Endangered, prior to the war, when a 1994 survey estimated that 16,900 Grauer's gorillas survived. By 2015, the estimated population was reduced to 3,800 Grauer's gorillas alive in the wild (Plumptre et al. 2016).

Both rebels and refugees have freely crossed these borders for decades. In small numbers, the environmental impact was primarily due to poaching, but damage on a massive scale occurred during the Rwandan genocide of 1994, in which some 800,000 people, mostly Tutsi, were massacred and nearly two million people, mostly Hutu, fled the country (Brauer 2009:123). This led to civil war in DRC that began in 1996. The refugee camps denuded large areas of forest, where desperate refugees sought firewood and building materials. In addition, armed militia and soldiers controlled small-scale mining in remote forest areas, and both miners and militia killed the gorillas, a prized meat.

THE CHEMISTRY OF WAR

While the military use of Agent Orange in Vietnam was not the first use of herbicides in war, it was the most extreme. The South Vietnamese began spraying herbicides obtained from the United States in 1961, killing vegetation to expose enemy troops. The practice continued under U.S. command until 1969. Agent Orange destroyed as much as half of South Vietnam's coastal mangrove forests. It degraded much of the inland tropical hardwood forests, which did not regenerate but turned into grassland and stands of bamboo. Anthropologists doing fieldwork in postwar Vietnam have pointed out that it was not only toxic chemicals but also wartime poverty that damaged forests and human health (Fox 2016; McElwee 2016).

Within the United States, neighborhoods located near toxic sites where chemical weapons were produced, stockpiled, and later destroyed were vulnerable to exposure. Most of this work was done under heavy secrecy in areas that had a peacetime chemical industry. Residents of West Anniston, Alabama, an African American community, had been exposed to polychlorinated biphenyls (PCBs) from the time when they were first manufactured in Anniston in 1930 until they were banned in the Toxic Substances Control Act of 1976. Monsanto manufactured PCBs primarily for use in insulation fluids, as in electrical transformers. PCBs were known from the 1960s to cause several slowly developing diseases such as liver cancer and to cause hormone disruption in infants and the offspring of other species, bioaccumulating in food chains and spreading globally. Older residents only learned of the levels of PCBs in their blood in the 1990s, after having been exposed to polluted air, soil, water, and fish from the creek in their neighborhood, not only during the years of production but continuing during the slow process of cleanup (Spears 2014).

During World Wars I and II, under cover of normal operation at its Anniston plant, Monsanto secretly produced chemical weapons for the

U.S. Army. Subsequently the Army ran its chemical and biological training there at Fort McClellan, adjacent to the city. The international Chemical Weapons Treaty that was drafted in 1992 and went into effect in 1997 outlawed the production, stockpiling, and use of chemical weapons. The ratification of the treaty set in motion a huge task of destroying these weapons. Fort McClellan closed in 1999, but construction went ahead on an incinerator to dispose of chemical weapons at the site.

One contribution of anthropologists and other social scientists has been to study the grassroots movements that arise out of situations like that in Anniston. The Calhoun County Improvement Association was originally organized around the civil rights issue of job discrimination in the 1970s, becoming a chapter of the Southern Christian Leadership Conference. Experience as civil rights activists served the residents well as they moved into the emerging issue of environmental justice in the 1990s, successfully demanding compensation for PCB-related illness and contaminated residential property (Spears 2014).

In addition to its stateside bases and former bases like Fort McClellan, the United States military also occupies 686 officially reported overseas bases. Sixty-four are active major military installations (Vine 2015:4). Most bases have substantial environmental impact, like any community of Americans. In addition, troops train with heavy petroleum-inefficient trucks, tanks, ships, and aircraft. Some bases are storage and practice sites for toxic weaponry. To develop a major base on the Indian Ocean island of Diego Garcia, the U.S. and UK deported the island's residents to Mauritius and the Seychelles, islands more than a thousand miles to the west (Vine 2009). Building the airfield and submarine base required clearing the island vegetation and blasting and dredging the coral reef.

The U.S. Navy used another island, Vieques, located off the eastern tip of Puerto Rico, as a live-ammunition training range for 60 years until local opposition intensified in the 1990s. The initial concern on Vieques was toxic contamination of drinking water, though protestors later addressed multiple issues (McCaffrey 2009). The island was named a Superfund site in 2004 and the Navy is still slowly cleaning up its dangerous wastes.

NUCLEAR WAR

The Manhattan Project began in 1942 to develop atomic bomb technology at many sites around the United States, each engaged in different parts of the project to enhance secrecy. The Los Alamos Laboratory in New Mexico built one type of nuclear device, the first atomic bomb in the world to be tested. It was tested at a site called Trinity in the Alamogordo Bombing and Gunnery Range in southern New Mexico

on July 16, 1945, and was the prototype for the bomb named "Fat Man"
that was dropped on Nagasaki, Japan, one month later, with the aim of
forcing the Japanese to surrender, faced with horrendous civilian casu-
alties. Another type of A-bomb, code-named "Little Boy," first exploded
at Hiroshima on August 6, 1945, was built in parts at several sites. The
immediate death of as many as 200,000 Japanese in these two 1945
bombings was the result of flying debris, burns, and radiation. In the
long term, many others would succumb to cancer. Thyroid cancer and
leukemia are sentinel malignancies most strongly associated with exposure to radiation from fallout. The Hanford site, in eastern Washington
State, which supplied the nuclear material for the American bombs,
was heavily polluted with radioactive waste that still requires expen-
sive cleanup and will remain lethal for generations (Liebow 2007).

Compared to Americans living near nuclear sites, the people near
Kazakhstan's test site of Semipalatinsk were even more heavily
exposed to radiation. This was the Soviet Union's primary aboveground and underground testing site from 1949 to 1989. Its high level
of secrecy kept workers on a nearby state farm unaware of the fact
that they were secretly being monitored for their radiation exposure.
When the site was closed, most workers moved away, but the ethnic
Kazakhs who descended from the nomadic herders indigenous to the
area remained. They subsist in poverty by breeding sheep, cows, and
horses. Although entering the former testing site is illegal, lack of
enforcement means that the animals graze on radioactive pastures.
The anthropologist working here found that the people, now aware of
their continuing exposure to low-level radiation, admit that the exposure makes everyone "a little sick" but imagine that their bodies are
somehow adapted to living in a radioactive ecosystem and that they
would die if they moved away (Stawkowski 2016:152).

After World War II, the United States acquired the Marshall
Islands, bringing three million square miles of the Pacific Ocean under
the control of the U.S. Navy as a United Nations Trust Territory. The
U.S. relocated residents of two atolls for a series of nuclear tests that
culminated on Bikini atoll in 1954 with the 15-megaton hydrogen
bomb "Bravo," estimated at one thousand times the force of the bombs
dropped on Hiroshima and Nagasaki. The entirety of the Marshall
Islands was downwind of testing, and hazardous levels of fallout were
measured on 28 atolls (Johnston and Barker 2008:28). The government evacuated residents of the closest one, Rongelap, after the explosion in 1954. Many of them returned to Rongelap in 1957, to live in
what turned out to be a still-hazardous marine and terrestrial ecosystem until 1985, when they were again removed from their customary
lands to live as renters on other islands. During these years on Rongelap the Brookhaven National Labs made them subjects of extensive
medical research. Many did develop thyroid problems, as expected.

These were treated, but there were many problems with the medical studies, which used an inappropriate control group consisting of persons now living on the island who had not experienced the Bravo blast. While officials continued to reassure them of their safety on the island from 1957 to 1985, residents noted other health consequences of their continuing exposure to radiation, particularly reproductive problems.

When the Marshall Islands Nuclear Claims Tribunal began to consider the payment of financial compensation for the losses that the people of Rongelap had experienced, it was clear than these losses extended well beyond the simple appraisal of their land and radiation-related illness. The Public Advocate for the Tribunal engaged two anthropologists, Barbara Rose Johnston and Holly Barker, as expert witnesses to conduct research from 1999 to 2001 with Rongalapese informants. Their 2001 report entered the public record as testimony for the Tribunal's judgment in 2007. This *Rongelap Report* became the centerpiece of their book *Consequential Damages of Nuclear War*, with discussion of its background and the challenges in seeking a meaningful remedy (Johnston and Barker 2008).

Within the continental United States, a hazard that continued even after the end of aboveground nuclear testing was the exposure of workers in uranium mines to radiation. As the military built up its stock of nuclear warheads for missiles and peacetime use of nuclear technology continued, uranium production peaked from 1948 to the 1980s. Even after arms competition with the USSR ceased, abandoned mines and mills remained an environmental hazard, not only in the American Southwest but near Indian reservations in Wyoming, South Dakota, Washington, and neighboring states (Moore-Nall 2015). Most of the uranium came from underground and open-pit mines in the Colorado Plateau area on and near Indian lands. Native Americans, especially Navajo miners and their families, were unknowingly exposed to cancer-causing doses of radiation through dust and drinking water.

More than 90 percent of the yellow uranium ore was processed in mills on or near Indian reservations, creating further toxic exposures that amount to environmental injustice. At the Church Rock uranium mill, located in New Mexico on private land bordering Navajo Tribal Trust Lands, 1,000 tons of radioactive mill waste and 93 million gallons of radioactive tailings breached a tailings dam in July 1979. The disaster contaminated the Puerco River water that Navajos and other farmers used for livestock and irrigation.

ENVIRONMENTAL CAUSES OF WAR

In this chapter, we have looked at the environmental consequences of warfare, but more often anthropologists have asked to what extent environmental change has been a significant *cause* of war. Archaeological excavations supply the long-term data that can address this question. At the Cowboy Wash community near Mesa Verde in southwest Colorado, for example, an extended period of severe drought began in A.D. 1130, as indicated by tree ring dating. The **bioarchaeologist** examining the skeletal materials from the site found evidence of violent injury and death beginning in that period, which she interpreted as the results of raids as food crops began to fail (Lambert 2013). By the end of the thirteenth century, Puebloan farmers abandoned the whole area.

On a much larger scale of death from conflict, global climate change is likely to become a major cause of war in the twenty-first century. It is clear to military analysts as well as to scientists that the severe drought that lasted from 2006 to 2011 was one of the complex of causes of civil war in Syria. During the drought, desperate farmers moved from rural areas to cities. Added to the large numbers of Iraqi refugees, displaced populations overwhelmed the ability of the economy, schools, hospitals, and other institutions in those cities to cope. By 2017, more than five million refugees had fled Syria.

RECOMMENDED READING

Barbara Rose Johnston, ed. 2007. *Half-Lives & Half-Truths: Confronting the Radioactive Legacies of the Cold War*. Santa Fe, NM: School for Advanced Research Press. Fifteen anthropologists listen to the experience of those who live with the consequences of America and Russia producing nuclear weapons.

RECOMMENDED FILMS

Adam Jonas Horowitz, director. 2011. *Nuclear Savage: The Islands of Secret Project 4.1*. 87 minutes. Portrays the Marshall Islanders and their response to the secret nuclear research conducted on them by the U.S. government.

Grant Aaker and Josh Wallaert, directors. 2007. *Arid Lands*. 102 minutes. Sidelong Films. Land and people of the Hanford nuclear site and Columbia River basin.

Sophie Rousmanier, director. 2013. *Yellow Fever: Uncovering the Navajo Uranium Legacy*. 54 minutes. America Reframed series. World Channel.org. Follows Tina Garnanez, a Navajo Army veteran, as she returns home and explores the effects of the history of uranium mining on her family.

Chapter Nine

The Climate Is Changing

Long ago, there was always ice all summer. You would see the [multiyear ice] all summer. Ice was moving back and forth this time of year. Now. No ice. Should be [multiyear]. You used to see that old ice coming from the west side of Sachs. No more. Now between Victoria Island and Banks Island, there is open water. Shouldn't be that way.
  —Frank Kudlak, Sachs Harbour, Canada, 1999 (Hassol 2004)

Across the Arctic, many indigenous people are observing the effects of climate change that are outside of the remembered experience of their cultures. Sea ice is changing and disappearing, affecting ringed seals and the polar bears that prey on them. Weather patterns are unpredictable and unstable, making sea travel more dangerous. Warm summers increase the numbers of biting flies and mosquitoes. More rain and the melting of permafrost make land travel more difficult. The thawing of permafrost has undermined the foundations of buildings, roads, and other infrastructure in Alaska, while coastal erosion has demolished homes and other buildings. These changes have happened rapidly in parts of the Arctic, though by far the largest share of human activities that accelerate climate change occur farther south in Canada and the United States, with their coal-burning power plants and gasoline-burning cars and trucks.

The small community of Sachs Harbour in the western Canadian Arctic initiated a research project to document local knowledge of climate change and to let the rest of the world know what was happening in their environment. The Inuvialuit of Sachs Harbour participated with cultural ecologists in a study that spanned the seasons during 1999 and 2000. In their seasonal round, they hunted musk ox and other animals in fall and winter, shifted to ice fishing on inland lakes in the spring, followed by the spring snow goose hunt. In the summer, during ice breakup, they hunted ringed seals from boats and off ice floes. Late summer was a time for fishing with gill nets (Nichols et al. 2004). Following the study, Arctic sea ice continued to shrink even more rapidly, as climatologists documented from satellite images since 1979.

Recording the traditional knowledge of Arctic peoples extends our understanding of climate change in the Arctic farther into the past, prior to the invention of technologies for mapping and measuring polar ice. Recording traditional knowledge also helps us to appreciate the changes to which Arctic peoples have had to adapt.

The anthropological perspective on climate change is distinctive from that of most other disciplines because anthropology includes prehistoric archaeology, enabling us to take a centuries-long view of cultural adaptation to climate change. The archaeological record shows that this is not the first time that Arctic peoples have had to adapt to a warming climate. In about A.D. 1000, a similar period of warming reduced the sea ice for a few centuries. In any time of drastic change there are winners and losers. The people of the Thule culture, hunters of the bowhead whale and other large sea mammals, were the winners, expanding throughout the North American Arctic and Greenland. The losers were the Palaeo-Eskimo people whose culture had developed in the region over a period of two thousand years. When the climate turned colder again and the bowhead whale was gone, the Thule people, ancestors of present-day Inuit, had to adapt to hunting smaller prey, such as caribou in the summer, ringed seal in the winter, and birds and fish in season. The seasonality of these resources meant that the Inuit had to become more mobile. Their adaptability and resilience allowed them to do this effectively, though in the twentieth century, access to schools, medical care, and other Euro-American institutions made it difficult to remain mobile, requiring adaptation to life in larger, settled communities once again (McElroy 2008, 2013).

RISING OCEANS, DISASTER-DISPLACED PEOPLE

Moving from the Arctic to tropical Polynesia, we encounter another leading edge of global climate change in the twenty-first century. The tiny country of Tuvalu is formed by a group of nine coral atolls located halfway between Hawaii and Australia. Its nearly 12,000 citizens became an independent nation in 1978, having formerly been linked with Kiribati as a British colony called the Gilbert and Ellice Islands. The island economy depends on fish, coconuts, and the remittances from emigrants who work in New Zealand or Fiji and as seamen on international shipping lines. Rising sea levels threaten Tuvalu with saltwater intrusion into the underground water table and increased vulnerability to flooding at spring tides and during storms (Chambers and Chambers 2001).

Pacific atoll dwellers are presented in the overseas media as potential "environmental refugees," that is, people who may be forced to relocate to New Zealand, Fiji, and other Pacific countries, due to environmental degradation. The designation "environmental refugee" is not helpful if it discourages investment in practical short-term measures for dealing with flooding, such as better land-use planning to avoid the most flood-prone areas. Another problem with the term "environmental refugee" is that, although their suffering is like that experienced by war refugees, most people displaced by environmental damage remain within their own nation. Calling them refugees suggests that they are outsiders rather than fellow citizens. This was true for the Americans displaced from New Orleans to neighboring states by Hurricane Katrina in 2005, who justly protested when the media referred to them as refugees (Masquelier 2006). The mention of Hurricane Katrina is a reminder that people living on atolls are only a fraction of the coastal populations that are affected by rising sea levels. Human modification has removed the natural barriers to storm surges once offered to coastlines by mangroves and wetlands.

One of the deepest global environmental injustices is that impoverished people, who contribute relatively small amounts of the greenhouse gases such as carbon dioxide and methane, already experience the worst effects of climate change. For example, the broad low coastal plain of Bangladesh is densely populated with rice farmers whose land would be submerged by a one-meter rise in sea level, placing the entire nation in food crisis. The effects of climate change are felt in Bangladesh through flooding from increasingly severe tropical cyclones such as the one in November 2007 that killed several thousand people and caused the evacuation of more than one million from their homes.

Not all flooding in Bangladesh is equally a disaster for all households, for Bangladesh depends on its annual floods to create and restore its fertile soils. The alluvial soil is earth eroded high in the Himalayas and deposited across the river delta. The agricultural system is adapted to the expectation of flooding. Farmers who can do so plant both flood- and drought-tolerant varieties of rice at different elevations and seasons to be ready for any eventuality. Poor farmers are less likely to have the land and labor available to do this, therefore, the poorest suffer most. Bangladeshi women are also more vulnerable than men to hazards such as flooding because they are in a poorer state of health and nutrition and, when living in female-headed households, are also likely to be impoverished. Political ecologists find that the distribution of power and wealth in a society is the major contributor to people's vulnerability to disaster (Blaikie 1994; Cannon 2002).

SKEPTICISM AND DENIAL

Citizens of other countries find it difficult to understand how so many Americans can express denial or doubt about *anthropogenic* climate change despite the scientific consensus on this matter. Polling around the time of the 2015 Paris climate talks confirmed that Americans were the slowest of countries to accept that global climate disruption was occurring or, if so, that this was an urgent problem or one that humans caused or could affect. Climate change is a "wicked problem" for policy makers, that is, one that is so complex that each attempt at a solution opens new levels to understand.

When public discussion of global warming in the United States began in the late 1980s, particularly in the hot summer of 1987, it was not a politicized issue, having been acknowledged by both parties, but by 1995, the Republican Party had seriously committed to challenge climate science as a basis for public policy. Fossil-fuel-industry-funded publicity campaigns hired the services of climate "contrarians," as anthropologist Myanna Lahsen calls them. Lahsen began to do ethnographic research among climate modelers in 1994, an example of science and technology studies (STS). Based at the U.S. National Center for Atmospheric Research (NCAR) in Boulder, Colorado, she studied general circulation models. These models generate predictions of how the climate will behave in the future depending on emissions of greenhouse gases. She found that some scientists at reputable institutions, mostly older ones trained in an earlier era of climate science, were skeptical of the highly complex computer models produced by younger scientists. However, she distinguishes moderate skepticism from a small group of extremist "contrarians." Most contrarians tend not to work in accredited universities or federal research labs, but they had outsized influence on public opinion through financial support from conservative organizations (Lahsen 2016).

Another ethnographer of climate scientists is Jessica O'Reilly, who began her STS research in Christchurch, New Zealand, among glaciologists, doing fieldwork in conferences, workshops, and offices. She also did fieldwork with the New Zealand researchers in Antarctica, camping on the Ross Island Shelf to work beside them. She compares the work of field scientists, computer modelers, and analysts of satellite imagery, all of whom are working to understand the behavior of the massive ice sheets and ice shelves of Antarctica as it contributes to future rise in sea level. Like Lahsen, she is concerned with how scientists present their findings to policy makers and the public. She continued this research by attending international conferences and by looking at multiple drafts of the Fourth Assessment of the Intergovernmental Panel on Climate Change and the reviewers' comments on them, pursuing such seemingly minor details as the fate of a simple typo to reveal the culture of climate science (O'Reilly 2016, 2017).

MOUNTAIN GLACIERS

While the amount of ice is much greater in Antarctica and Greenland than in mountain glaciers, it is melting more slowly. The mountain glaciers that add so much beauty to the summits of continental mountains are shrinking at varying rates; they are retreating at least 10 meters each year on average. Tourist spots such as Mount Kilimanjaro of Kenya and Glacier Park in Montana and ski resorts in the Alps have lost more of their ice than can be replenished each winter by snow. An indigenous Quechua elder of the Peruvian Andes expressed the aesthetic and spiritual aspect of this change by saying:

> Our Apus (sacred mountain deities) have always had sparkling white ponchos. Now some of their ponchos have brown stripes. Other peaks have shed their ponchos altogether. (quoted in Bolin 2009)

The initial impact of melting glaciers is a downstream increase in summer floods. The long-range impact is the lack of water for irrigation agriculture on which peasant farmer/herders at high altitudes and commercial farms downstream depend. Hydroelectric power and drinking water supplies are also threatened.

The control of water is enmeshed in social and ecological relationships that can be extremely complex, differing even from village to village. Each village in highland Peru expects to have its own irrigation channel. Water governance is a combination of bottom-up village politics, top-down state control, the remnants of the old regime of wealthy large landowners, and conflicts over the water demands of mining development (Rasmussen 2015).

DISASTER, HAZARD, AND RISK

Hazard is the most general term for a source of danger of death or injury. *Risk* is a closely related term, adding the element of chance or probability. A disaster is an extreme manifestation of risk, concentrated in time or place. The boundaries between disasters and ordinary, recurrent forms of risk are fuzzy. We perceive a plane crash with 130 lives lost as a disaster but do not call more than seven million deaths per year from smoking a disaster. The deaths from chronic diseases exacerbated by smoking are spread out in time and space. Even so, smoking is much more risky behavior than flying, in statistical terms.

Most disasters are located somewhere in the middle of a continuum between the natural and the social. The death of 500,000 people in 1988 in a famine in Sudan had a natural component in drought, but the shortage of food in the rebellious southern and western parts of the country was largely engineered by the Khartoum government for political and economic purposes. Had it chosen to do so, the government could have prevented many deaths by allowing available food to be distributed (Keen 1994). Lax enforcement of building codes increases the death toll when victims are crushed or trapped by earthquakes. "Natural" disasters such as drought and earthquake are thus inextricably bound up with the social and political.

As global warming increases, in addition to elevated mortality rates during heat waves, more extreme weather events combined with population growth lead to more significant disasters in vulnerable populations. Therefore, anthropologists have increasingly turned their attention to describing and analyzing disasters and the response to them. From a 1972 earthquake causing a massive landslide burying his field site, the city of Yungay, Peru, anthropologist Anthony Oliver-Smith (2013) turned to the study of hurricanes in Florida and to disaster resilience more generally. Gregory Button (2010) was concerned with a series of disasters occurring within the fossil-fuel industries, such as the Exxon oil spill in Alaska, an even larger oil spill in the Shetland Islands in the North Sea, and a coal ash spill in 2008 in Tennessee.

In environmental anthropology, we are interested in how societies manage the hazards to which they are prone. How do high-altitude farmers in Papua New Guinea prepare their fields and diversify their plantings for the occasional but infrequent frost? How do Americans establish the locations for hazardous waste dumps? How do the livestock herders of East Africa manage to get through extended times of drought?

COPING WITH DROUGHT

The Ariaal pastoralists of northern Kenya are one such group who were studied through good times and bad by an environmental anthropologist, Elliot Fratkin, who began his study of the Ariaal in 1971 and returned to Kenya several times (Fratkin 2004). The Ariaal population of about 10,000 follows a mixture of two cultural traditions—the Rendille, speaking a Cushitic language related to Somali, and the Samburu, speaking a Nilotic language related to the language of the Maasai. Fratkin observed that an average Ariaal household of five people kept 12 camels, 20 cattle, and 50 sheep and goats. The herds provided milk, making up 70 percent of the Ariaal diet daily, and occasionally meat and blood for food. Animals were also sold to purchase grain, sugar, and tea.

The different species in the herd behave differently, making it important to keep a diversity of animals. Goats and camels browse on twigs and leaves, while sheep and cattle prefer to eat grass. Camels are good milk producers but have a low population growth rate because of a low number of births and the death of their young to infectious disease and parasites. Sheep and goats reproduce more quickly, so they are important for building up a herd after a drought. Cattle are most vulnerable to drought, which has returned every four or five years since 1968. During the long drought that lasted from 1982 to 1984 the Ariaal lost more than 50 percent of their cattle.

The Ariaal strategy for coping with hazards was to keep large numbers of different stock, to maximize herd size, and to disperse their herds in different areas. They did this by lending animals to friends and kin far away, where conditions were different. Mobility used to be an important strategy but was lost as grazing land came under pressure from population growth, the expansion of agriculture, and the creation of commercial ranches and game parks. Under severe conditions, the former mechanisms for coping with drought were not easy to sustain. The most impoverished Ariaal families were driven out of pastoralism and into town, where they depended on famine relief agencies or odd jobs.

Anthropologists working among other nomadic population of herders in Kenya indicate that not everyone responds in the same way to changing circumstances. This diversity of response is one of the factors that helps a socio-ecological system persist through drought and other challenges; that is, variation contributes to resilience (Leslie and McCabe 2013). Within social networks, for example of brothers and brothers-in-law, different men had herds of different composition, reducing risk by helping each other out when one of them failed. However, the droughts caused by future climate change may well exceed the resilience of nomadic herders.

THE QUESTION OF THE COMMONS

Many of the resources we consider in this text—Indonesian and Mexican forests, hunting rights to sea mammals, water for irrigation, grazing lands—are not privately owned. Instead they are held in common by a group of people, small or large. Ecologist Garrett Hardin proposed the influential theory of "the tragedy of the commons" in 1968. Hardin's view was based on the old English commons, a shared pasture. Hardin asserted that each herdsman will selfishly keep on adding more cows to his herd because he gets the full benefits of each cow and calf while the whole community shares the costs of overgrazing, the damage to the pasture.

Economists further developed Hardin's model, arguing that only private property could protect resources. In this bleak view, humans are doomed to overpopulate and degrade the environment because individuals will inevitably choose their private advantage over the common good. Anthropologists criticized the individualistic bias of the commons model, showing that property rights around the world are much more complex (McCay and Acheson 1987). Traditionally, people have succeeded in managing common-pool resources in sustainable ways. "Common property" does not mean that everybody has open access; instead societies have systems of rights, duties, and obligations that protect resources held in common. Furthermore, owners of private property do not always behave in ecologically responsible ways either, often discounting future use in favor of present gain.

Anthropologists have often focused on local cases such as the Inuvialuit of Canada and the Ariaal of Kenya, but the environmental hazards that we now face are related to common-pool resources on an international or global scale. These include such resources as the fresh water of the Great Lakes on the U.S.–Canadian border and tropical rain forests whose existence affects the global climate, atmosphere, and oceans. The magnitude of these problems reflects a world population whose growth has accelerated, now surpassing seven billion.

RECOMMENDED READING

Gregory Button. 2010. *Disaster Culture: Knowledge and Uncertainty in the Wake of Human and Environmental Catastrophe.* Walnut Creek, CA: Left Coast Press. As anthropologist and former journalist, Button clarifies the way that corporate and public officials spin the story of environmental catastrophes.
Susan Alexandra Crate and Mark Nuttall, eds. 2016. *Anthropology and Climate Change: From Actions to Transformations.* 2nd ed. New York: Routledge, Taylor & Francis. Edited collection of papers by anthropologists working on the major topics in contemporary climate change from Chesapeake Bay to Siberia.
Al Gore. *The Climate Reality Project.* Resources on the basics of climate change, including an editable PowerPoint presentation. https://www.climaterealityproject.org/
J. Terence McCabe. 2004. *Cattle Bring Us to Our Enemies: Turkana Ecology, Politics, and Raiding in a Disequilibrium System.* Ann Arbor: University of Michigan Press. As a team member of one of the largest multidisciplinary ecological studies, the South Turkana Ecosystem Project, McCabe studied four Kenyan pastoralist families in depth.

RECOMMENDED FILMS

Bonnie Dickie, et al. 2000. *Sila Alangotok: Inuit Observations on Climate Change.* 42 minutes. Winnepeg: International Institute of Sustainable Development. Sachs Harbour residents discuss changes they had already seen by the beginning of this century.
Ross Harrison. 2016. *Facing the Mountain.* 20 minutes. Resilience of people of a Himalayan valley in North India following a flood in 2013. https://facingthemountain.com/
Seth Kramer, Daniel A. Miller, and Jeremy Newberger, directors. 2015. *The Anthropologist.* 78 minutes. Ironbound Films. Anthropologist Susan Crate and her daughter visit indigenous people affected by climate change.
David MacDougall, James Blue, and Paul Baxter, directors. 1974 (digitally remastered 2017). *Boran Herdsmen.* 18 minutes. Documentary Educational Resources/Faces of Change series. Depicts cattle herding practices of the Boran in Kenya.

Chapter Ten

Population
and Environment

In October 2011 the population of the world passed seven billion. There were signs that the rate of reproduction had leveled off slightly, but the momentum of children already born growing to adulthood and having children of their own assured that the population would not stop growing anytime soon.

Anthropologists are trained to take the long view on the big questions. World population is one of those big questions. It had taken only 40 years for world population to double, going from three billion in 1960 to six billion in 1998. Back in 1850, in the middle of the Industrial Revolution, the world population was only one billion. At the beginning of agriculture in the Middle East about 10,000 years ago, world population was probably somewhere between five and ten million. In comparison, by 2016 there were 30 megacities, each with a population of more than ten million.

This long sweep of human population history forms the background for all of anthropology and its subdisciplines. Prehistoric archaeologists, for instance, have attempted to identify evidence left behind by tiny populations of hunter-gatherers soon after they entered new continents, such as Australia and North America. Cultural anthropologists and biological anthropologists studying contemporary hunter-gatherers have cautiously used them as models of population processes of fertility and mortality in ancient foraging societies. Linguistic anthropologists have tracked the migration of the Polynesians into the islands of the Pacific by showing how related languages diverged over the past several centuries. Applied anthropologists, working as consultants in family planning programs, have investigated what motivates families in Indonesia or India to accept or reject contraceptives. Population is relevant to a wide variety of questions.

COLLAPSE

One of the great puzzles of archaeology is the buildup and subsequent collapse of the great Maya civilization that occupied the lowland tropical forests stretching from Mexico's Yucatan Peninsula through Belize and Guatemala to Honduras. Impressive ceremonial centers such as Tikal and Copán reached their peak in the Late Classic period between AD 700 and 800. The central authority collapsed and the elaborate structures fell into disuse long before the Spanish conquerors arrived.

The rise and fall of Maya civilization can be tracked as a rise and fall of population. One of the best-studied of the Classic Maya centers is Copán in western Honduras. The urban center of Copán contained a palace complex where the king and nobles lived and an elaborate collection of pyramids, temples, tombs, and sculptures. At its peak population, between AD 750 and 900, the city may have had as many as 10,000 to 12,000 people living in one square kilometer. A similar number lived in settlements scattered throughout the Copán valley. From its peak, totaling at least 20,000, the population began dropping. By AD 1000 it had diminished to about 7,500 people, and by AD 1200 to about 1,000 people. Soon after this, the area was virtually abandoned. As dramatic as this crash sounds, until recent studies were complete, archaeologists thought the peak population was even larger and the crash even more abrupt (Andrews and Fash 2005; Webster 2002; Webster, Freter, and Gonlin 2000).

How do archaeologists know what the population of these ancient Maya centers was in different eras? The Maya had hieroglyphic writing but did not, as far as we know, keep censuses. The main clue to population size is counting the number and size of structures occupied during each period. The periods, or phases, of occupation are usually defined by changes in pottery style. The house-count method requires assuming the average number of persons per household, typically between four and six persons for a family. A second method uses computer simulations of the agricultural productivity of the soils under cultivation at each period. These methods are indirect enough that controversy remains about the extent of population decline. In some Maya areas outside the Copán valley, there does not appear to have been a population decline so much as a scattering of people out over the countryside away from the urban centers.

The prevailing explanation for the Maya collapse at Copán has been an ecological one. According to this model, the downfall came about because the people attempted to live on slash-and-burn maize cultivation in a tropical lowland environment under increasing population pressure. Drought was possibly a factor, though the timing of drought in relation to collapse does not square well with this explanation. Deforestation, the invasion of grasses, soil depletion, and erosion cut into productivity, ultimately causing nutrition and health to deteriorate. People became more vulnerable to infectious and parasitic diseases, especially those causing diarrhea, and the dense settlement helped these diseases to spread.

At the time of the conquest the Spanish observed that slash-and-burn single-crop maize fields were the only form of subsistence in the severely depopulated Maya region. But archaeologists now know that at the peak of population, the Maya were practicing more intensive farming. They built raised fields in wetlands and constructed terraces to manage water and soil fertility. This increased sophistication in farming does not mean that the Maya did not degrade the environment, although it does give us a new respect for their agricultural knowledge.

The archaeologists who have uncovered house platforms and pots are not the only anthropologists who have contributed to an understanding of the population and environment of the Maya. Bioarchaeologists study the bones and teeth in ancient burials. The Maya buried their dead under the floors of individual houses. With no big cemeteries to give large samples of skeletons, it is a slow process to build up a picture of changing health conditions across time, place, and social status. Some of this skeletal evidence does support the ecological hypothesis. Comparing the length of leg bones, for example, suggests that, on average, men were shorter in later time periods. As the population grew, food may have become scarce, stunting growth. Defects in the enamel of children's teeth also support the conclusion that Maya health deteriorated over time. The teeth show that children experienced significant nutritional stress around age three, the usual age of weaning. In the Late Classic period at Copán, children buried in a relatively wealthy residential group were under nutritional and infectious disease stress (Storey 1992).

Few anthropologists find the ecological explanation for the Maya decline by itself fully satisfying, and they add a political dimension to their explanations. In the case of Copán, for example, the last kings lost their grip on the kingdom. Privileged people, the nobles, were increasingly powerful and continued to have access to valuable imported goods such as pottery for deposit in their own tombs, even after the construction of royal monuments ceased. Royal power collapsed abruptly, but it is not clear whether the final blow to it came from internal political conflict or external war. There is little indication from trauma to skeletons or the sudden destruction of buildings that there was mass violence at the time of the so-called "collapse." Population remained high for a while after the political crisis and then began to decline.

Cahokia is a North American site that collapsed long before the devastating arrival of colonists from Europe. It was the largest of the ritual centers of the Mississippian chiefdoms that stretched from southern Illinois through Alabama and Georgia. The massive Cahokia complex of mounds and plazas was built across the Mississippi River from present-day St. Louis, Missouri. It remained the major ritual center for its region from about 900 to 1200 C.E., when its estimated population reached 20,000. It scaled back for a century, and by 1400 C.E. it had been abandoned. The reason for the meltdown may have been deforestation and resulting erosion of the surrounding hills, as was suggested for Copán, or again it may have been the emergence of political factions and influences from cultural traditions from the north (Kelly 2008).

DEMOGRAPHIC ANTHROPOLOGY

Unlike archaeologists, cultural anthropologists can and routinely do take a census of the communities in which they do their fieldwork. This is usually one of the first things that a new fieldworker does to get acquainted. I found that I needed to take a daily census in my small Papua New Guinea village because people were constantly coming and going. Although their numbers are tiny on a world scale, the demography of the nomadic or seminomadic hunters and foragers has been taken as a possible clue to how the human population remained low for so many generations. The !Kung San, hunter-foragers of the Kalahari Desert of southern Africa, are the classic example. Women, unable to carry more than one child while *foraging* for plant foods, experience moderate fertility, prolonged breast feeding, and long spacing between births (Howell 1979).

Tom and Janet Headland accumulated detailed census data during their first 40 years as missionary-linguists with the Agta Negritos of the Philippines. Analysis of the data showed how the Agta hunter-gatherers were being assimilated into the lowland farming society by migration and intermarriage. During this phase of their history, the Agta experienced high fertility and infant mortality and an alarmingly short life expectancy averaging 23 years (Early and Headland 1998).

Another thoroughly investigated population of forest foragers are the Northern Aché of Paraguay. Just before the Northern Aché came into peaceful contact with the outside world at mission settlements after decades of violent conflict with peasant colonists, their population was about 540. Immediately after contact, the population declined by one-third to one-half because of epidemic diseases to which the Aché did not have immunity. Because so many of the survivors were young adults, the population rebounded quickly to 552 in 1997 despite a high prevalence of tuberculosis (Hill and Hurtado 1996; Hurtado et al. 2003).

POPULATION GROWTH AND
ENVIRONMENTAL DEGRADATION IN HONDURAS

Environmentalists make a simple and powerful argument about the relationship between population growth and environmental impact. It is summed up in the equation

Impact = Population × Affluence × Technology

The IPAT equation was popularized in the book *The Population Explosion* (Ehrlich and Ehrlich 1990). This makes sense in relation to the United States, for example, with the third-largest population of any nation, great affluence, and technology that is heavily based on the internal combustion engine. This combination of population size and consumption means that the United States has a huge impact on the global environment.

Applying the IPAT equation to the developing world suggests that if more people succeed in their aspiration to live at the same level of affluence as in the United States, the impact on the environment will be severe. Unless the developing countries slow the growth of their population and choose less damaging technologies, the quality of life for everyone will suffer. The IPAT equation is a good commonsense argument. Nevertheless, it is one that anthropologists find inadequate because it oversimplifies the processes at work in the human impact on the environment.

The Central American countries provide a clear instance of environmental degradation that cannot be understood simply as a direct result of local population growth multiplied by affluence and technology. This is so even in the most rapidly growing country in the region, Honduras, a mountainous tropical country of eight million people that traditionally exported bananas and coffee (Durham 1995; Stonich 1993).

The forests of Honduras were cut to create pastures to feed cattle during the beef boom of the 1960s and 1970s. The beef was largely exported rather than fed to the growing local population. When the cattle boom ended in the early 1980s, the Honduran government encouraged the development of nontraditional export foods, especially melons and shrimp. Both these new exports were environmentally damaging. Melon farmers used high levels of pesticides. Shrimp farmers cultivated shrimp in large ponds developed in coastal wetlands, damaging coastal mudflats and mangrove ecosystems. Road building and the buildup of sediments caused further problems. The private development of shrimp farms cut off public access to fishing grounds, reducing an important source of food for local people.

These environmental impacts are not a simple result of population growth. Anthropologists who seek to understand the degradation of the environment in Central America point to the inequality of access to resources as the basic cause of environmental degradation. Market demand encourages the rich to expand the commercial production of beef cattle, cotton, melons, palm oil, and other export products. This leads to deforestation and to the further concentration of land ownership when they buy up more land with their profits. The poor are pushed off these lands. Further impoverished, they intensify their own household production, using marginal lands such as those higher up the mountain slopes. These marginal lands then become deforested and eroded. Erosion exposes the slopes to the increased likelihood of landslides during the heavy rains that come with hurricanes. The rich get richer and the poor get poorer in two positive feedback loops, both of which lead to more deforestation.

While inequality of access is a much more fundamental problem in Honduras than population growth, this is not to say that population growth is unrelated to environmental degradation. Indeed, Honduran poverty encourages population growth. Larger families provide child labor in poor households and cheap labor for the new developments.

Honduran environmental degradation deleteriously affects human health. The indiscriminate use of agricultural pesticides on fields of export crops destroyed the predators of the whitefly, and the whitefly transmits a viral disease to beans. Damage to the bean crop, on which the poor depend for protein, led to increases in child malnutrition (Almendares et al. 1993). The use of agricultural pesticides also led to widespread resistance to insecticides by mosquitoes, spreading malaria and dengue, and sand flies spreading the infectious skin disease leishmaniasis. In the next chapter, we will look at other ways in which the loss of biodiversity affects human health.

RECOMMENDED READING

Nora Haenn, Richard Wilk, and Allison Harnish, eds. 2016. *The Environment in Anthropology: A Reader in Ecology, Culture, and Sustainable Living.* 2nd ed. New York: NYU Press. Forty-two readings complement the later chapters of this book with their focus on population, sustainability, toxic waste, conservation of biodiversity, globalization, and consumerism.

Gyles Iannone, ed. 2014. *The Great Maya Droughts in Cultural Context: Case Studies in Resilience and Vulnerability.* Boulder: University Press of Colorado. Fifteen papers by 36 archaeologists critically assess the collapse model for ancient Maya civilization from current ecological models.

RECOMMENDED FILM

Marc Francis and Nick Francis, directors/producers. 2006. *Black Gold.* (78 minutes). Speakit. Follows an Ethiopian farmer as he travels the world attempting to get a fair price for his high-quality coffee beans.

Chapter Eleven

Biodiversity and Health
in the Anthropocene

W e are in the midst of the sixth mass extinction in the history of our planet, the first one caused by humans. The expansion of the human population is taking vast amounts of land habitat away from other creatures. Our use of fossil energy releases greenhouse gases into the atmosphere and warms and acidifies the oceans, destroying coral reef habitats with their rich biodiversity. This combination of events led to the proposal to name our geological epoch the *Anthropocene*, the era in which humans are the main force shaping geology. (Because the wealthiest nations, corporations, and people are responsible for most of the impact, the term "Capitalocene" would be more accurate.) In earlier chapters, we have alluded to other features of the Anthropocene. For example, mining reshapes planetary geology: digging big holes, moving large amounts of sediment, and refining and moving metals to urban areas and rubbish heaps.

A global geological marker for the start of the epoch is the radioactive fallout from the burst of nuclear tests during the 1950s. The period after 1950 is known as "the great acceleration" because a steep increase in human population from two billion in 1950 to seven billion in 2011 was accompanied by economic growth and steep increases in solid waste, soil erosion, carbon emissions, and a host of other environmental indicators such as decreases in the population size and habitat area of many species of wildlife.

The word *biodiversity* most often refers to the abundance of species, and loss of biodiversity refers to the extinction of species. Biologists have described and named more than two million species out of what they currently estimate to be about 8.7 million species of animals, plants, algae, fungi, and the more complex of the microorganisms. Many species will become extinct before they are discovered; for example, frogs are especially vulnerable while also poorly known to biologists (Wilson 2016). The loss of the insects, birds, and bats that have specialized relationships with plants for pollination and seed dispersal is particularly worrisome, for it would cause a cascade of other extinctions.

The species level is not the only level at which biodiversity is important. Above the species level, there is a diversity of ecosystems or landscapes, larger units that can collapse or disappear. Below the species level, there is genetic diversity within each species to be preserved or lost. One kind of biodiversity that is particularly important to humans is the variation within species of crop plants. Since the origin of agriculture some 10,000 years ago, farmers have carefully maintained at least small plantings of many varieties of important food crops such as rice or potatoes. Each variety has its own special qualities, such as resistance to a pest, a desired flavor or texture, or an attractive color. Different varieties thrive in slightly different microenvironments under specific conditions of soil, water, and temperature. Especially since the Green Revolution and the more recent development of genetically modified crop varieties, the genetic diversity of crop plants has been threatened. If this diversity is lost, we will not have the genetic materials that will be needed to breed improved plants in the future as insurance against climate change or new plant diseases.

Virginia Nazarea, an anthropologist doing research on agricultural decision making in the Philippines, became concerned that local knowledge connected to these older varieties of crop plants would soon die out. Working with rice farmers in Bukidnon province on the island of Mindanao, she began to document the indigenous beliefs and practices associated with sweet potato cultivation. She called this "memory banking," in contrast to gene banking that preserves only the genetic variability, and helped develop a plan to keep growing the heirloom varieties in local gardens and not only at agricultural research stations (Nazarea 1998).

THREATS TO BIODIVERSITY

Despite the pleasure that humans often take in diversity—for example, in dog breeds ranging from Chihuahuas to Great Danes—we are also the most important threat to biodiversity. Hunters were responsible for the extinction of large animal species throughout the world toward the end of the Ice Age (Martin and Klein 1984; Sandom et al. 2014). The extinction of mammals such as the mammoth and giant beaver was not likely due to climate change alone because the extinctions occurred at different times in different continents, following the entrance of humans. Humans rarely drive other species to extinction by hunting, however. Instead, we destroy and fragment habitats and introduce exotic species that compete with native species.

Ecological anthropologists have become adept in the use of new technologies such as remote sensing and geographic information systems (GIS) to document changes in land use and land cover. The intensification of agriculture and the loss of forest cover are important changes that need to be studied at different levels, from the household to the region to the global scale (Moran 2008).

The introduction of exotic species may be equally disastrous whether it is accidental or intentional. The Polynesians inadvertently introduced rats to Rapa Nui (Easter Island), for example, accidentally bringing them along in their canoes as they traveled. Archaeologists debate who bears more responsibility for the deforestation of the island and extinction of the *Jubaea* palm: people who cut palms as rollers to move huge statues from the quarries or rats that gnawed on the palm seeds and kept them from germinating. In either case, deforestation occurred well before the demographic and cultural collapse that was caused by disease and slave trading following European contact (Hunt and Lipo 2011).

Australians intentionally introduced cane toads from South and Central America to Australia in 1935, hoping to control beetles in the sugar cane fields. The poisonous toads failed to control the beetles but depleted the population of blue-tongue lizards, goannas, and other animals that aboriginal women hunted for food (Seton and Bradley 2004).

MEDICINAL PLANTS

Another way that the loss of biodiversity threatens health is through the loss of medicinal plants. Many effective medicines obtained from plants have been known from ancient times. One that is still used is quinine, a malaria treatment that is obtained from cinchona bark, the bark of a South American tree. Quinine gained renewed importance after malaria parasites developed resistance to newer drugs. Then, after quinine became less effective because of resistance, treatment shifted to another drug obtained from an ancient Chinese plant remedy, artemisinin. Digitalis for the heart is a constituent of the foxglove, a northern European flowering plant. Twentieth-century plant medicine discoveries include most famously treatments for cancer derived from the Madagascar rosy periwinkle and from the yew tree of the Pacific Northwest (Walsh and Goodman 2002).

Many important medicinal plants come from tropical forests; hence part of the threat of logging these forests is that the source of future pharmaceuticals may be lost. The significance of tropical forests as a source of medicines is not merely coincidental but is related to ecology. The tropics contain a disproportionate percentage of the total number of species. In addition, insects and microorganisms thrive year-round, without a seasonal check during cold weather. Tropical plants have evolved a host of biochemical defenses against these pests. Many of these substances show chemical activity that is useful to modern medicine and agriculture.

Multinational drug companies do bioprospecting, deriving clues from the medicinal plants traditionally used by forest peoples. This is a shortcut to choose the plants to screen first. The companies analyze these for active compounds, test them, and then develop synthetic derivatives so that they do not need to rely on importing supplies gathered from the forest. There is also a profitable market for herbals that have not undergone this full process of testing and synthesis to qualify as drugs but are sold as dietary supplements in health stores.

Research to find new plant medicines is actively carried on by drug companies, universities, botanical gardens, and government laboratories. Anthropologists have little role in the laboratory side of this process. Their research role is in the field—documenting the context of plant use and studying ethnomedicine by observing and interviewing healers, shamans, midwives, and their patients. Anthropologists serve as advocates for the right of indigenous people to share in the profits to be gained from drug discoveries, whether the discoveries stem from traditional healers' knowledge or simply from the plants collected from their lands (Posey and Dutfield 1996; Sillitoe 2006). The difficulty of attaining justice in highly politicized research settings has unfortunately forced some ethnobotanists to give up doing this kind of fieldwork to avoid controversy.

EMERGING INFECTIOUS DISEASES

The loss of medicinal plant species is only one facet of rapid environmental change. The same forces for change expose human populations to new infectious diseases. Population growth pushes agriculture and settlements to move into new areas. During this expansion, predator populations are reduced through habitat loss and the use of pesticides. These predators might otherwise have kept rodents and insects in check. The expanding populations of rodents and insects may cause crops to be lost or serve as *vectors* for the spread of infectious disease.

As human populations enter new, marginal areas, they may contact vectors and *reservoirs* of new infectious diseases for which they have no immunity. Medical anthropologists illustrate this series of events with Kyasanur Forest disease. This disease, caused by a *virus* spread by ticks, had long been present at low levels in India, but an epidemic broke out after extensive clearing of the forest for an economic development project brought people in closer contact with ticks (Nichter 1987).

Global climate change that alters ecosystems affects human health, for example, by allowing mosquito vectors to spread malaria and other diseases at higher altitudes. In the American Northeast and Upper Midwest, climate change has contributed to an increase in Lyme disease, a bacterial disease spread by ticks. Of course, climate change affects human health more directly through heat exhaustion that causes illness or death, particularly among the elderly (USEPA 2016).

Changes in marine ecosystems of the warm coastal waters offshore from Peru, India, and Bangladesh led to cholera epidemics in the 1990s. Damaged marine ecosystems are simplified ecosystems lacking the biodiversity that maintains stability, and unstable conditions favor small organisms that multiply rapidly. Many of these are toxic or pathogenic, for example, the bacteria that cause cholera. Warmer sea temperatures and pollution increase the growth of algae among which cholera vibrios thrive.

Ebola is the *emerging disease* most in the news with outbreaks in several West African nations in 2014–2016, following outbreaks in central African countries in earlier years. The initial, or index, case seems to have been a two-year old boy playing in a hollow tree in Guinea containing a colony of insect-eating bats. The child then transmitted the virus to his family as they cared for him until he died. Subsequently most transmission was the result of the poor health care system of the affected countries. Many of the victims were hospital workers. Others were residents of crowded, impoverished urban neighborhoods. Even though human-to-human transmission was the rule after the index case, health messages and rumors led people to stop consuming game meat, although there was not any real risk in eating cooked meat (Ngade et al. 2016).

People hunting and butchering game are normally most exposed to viruses carried by game animals. However, observations by an anthropologist of shared contact with raw food between humans and other primates led her to initiate an interdisciplinary research project to examine other possibilities for animal–human and human–animal transmission. She observed a Sierra Leonean walking through a forest snack on ripe fruit that had been gnawed by chimpanzees. Chimps raiding gardens also may have left their saliva or other body fluids on foods later harvested by the garden's owners (Bolten 2016). Diseases that have colonies of bats as their reservoir without causing the bats much trouble may cause fatal outbreaks in both humans and gorillas or chimpanzees.

Much of this chapter could well be considered to belong to medical anthropology rather than environmental anthropology. There is a necessary overlap between these two subdisciplines. Many of the health problems that people experience need to be understood by considering the environmental hazards to which they are exposed (McElroy and Townsend 2015). Often these environmental hazards are clustered in *syndemics*, that is, diseases and health conditions that are more deleterious by occurring together, often in impoverished and powerless individuals or communities (Singer 2009).

Physician anthropologist Paul Farmer (2004) borrowed the term "structural violence" from liberation theology to refer to the oppression built into a social order characterized by poverty and steep grades of social inequality, including racism and gender inequality. Structural violence is violence that is exerted systematically by everyone who belongs to a certain social order, indirectly, without their necessarily intending or being aware of doing so. Because so much ill health is the result of structural violence, many medical anthropologists identify their discipline as the political ecology of health, seeking to explore the pathways by which inequality damages health.

ASSESSING RISK

Hazards are sometimes referred to as risks to emphasize that there is an element of probability associated with their occurring in a given period of time. This probability can be expressed mathematically, adding precision to the term risk. Engineers speak of designing a dam for a "hundred-year flood," meaning that the magnitude of a flood that will overtop the dam can be expected to occur, on average, once every hundred years. (Of course, they cannot tell you whether that will be next year or the year 2050! That is the element of chance.) Insurance companies and gamblers are also concerned with the probability of certain events.

In societies with specializations such as engineering and insurance underwriting, laypeople evaluate risk differently than specialists in risk analysis. Laypersons consider not only the size and probability of risk but questions of fairness, equity, and a sense of control. Cultural differences lead them to select some dangers for public concern while downplaying others. Furthermore, people do not often have all the information they need to make rational, informed decisions because powerful institutions such as corporations and governments control such knowledge and use it to manage people's responses. This was the case at the Ok Tedi Mine, where the mining company published a glossy public relations brochure, reassuring people that the mine was environmentally harmless, only to reverse itself later.

To reduce public anxiety, bureaucrats often issue reassuring statements until they can clarify what the dangers are. These reassurances sometimes deny people information they need to make good decisions. Anthropologist Gregory Button (1995) discovered this in studying the public health response to a Shetland Islands oil spill in 1993 from a tanker in the North Sea, between Scotland and Norway. Button had earlier studied the *Exxon Valdez* oil spill in Alaska. The Shetland Islands spill, though less publicized than the Alaskan one, involved twice as much oil. The spraying of toxic chemical dispersants that were used to clean up the oil spill contaminated agricultural land, sheep, cattle, and people. Residents were given inadequate warning, and their health was not adequately monitored. Had they known more, they could at least have stayed indoors and reduced their exposure to the toxic sprays.

Their employers did not inform the Navajo uranium workers discussed in Chapter 8 of the risks of radiation that led to lung cancer. Because it was a slowly developing disease, many persons, including family members exposed to clothing and equipment brought home by workers, developed cancer before they learned of the danger.

The lack of relevant and timely information after a disaster hurts some groups more than others. Young mothers in the small rural communities near the Fukushima Daiichi nuclear power plant faced the hardest decisions in the years following the March 2011 disaster when a tsunami destroyed the power plant. While they felt pressures to support the economic recovery of their communities, they needed to leave to protect their children's health from radiation (Slater and Morioka 2014). The chief threat after nuclear accidents is cesium-137, a long-lived lethal fission product that is released as a gas from the used fuel rods that are stored at power plants. As the cesium falls from the air with rain it makes its way into water and soil and is taken up into plants and people, where it damages DNA, causing cancer, genetic mutations, and birth defects.

Different groups of stakeholders may come into conflict because they assess risks in disparate ways. In rapidly industrializing China, for example, air and water pollution are extreme. The largest share of pollution is emitted in rural factories such as the zinc smelter in the small township of Futian in Sichuan province. These rural factories burn dirty coal without employing technologies for mitigating its environmental impact. Enforcement of environmental regulations is lax in rural areas. All occupational groups acknowledge that industrial pollution poses many risks: direct influences on human and animal health, damage to crops and to the food chain, and threats to longevity. (Long life is a significant cultural value in China.) Factory workers, many of them migrants new to the area, are more likely to downplay the risks to health and longevity than either farmers or service workers (Tilt 2006).

People in all cultures must make many important decisions with inadequate information about the environment. The tropical forest is a particularly complex system with too many variables of soil, water, vegetation, pests, and weather to predict reliably the outcome of plantings. Under some circumstances the best decision, the one least likely to lead to a crop failure from floods, dry spells, pests, or other hazards, is to flip a coin, that is, to randomize. This is true in selecting new sites for swiddens in Borneo. As the Kantu' of West Kalimantan (Indonesian Borneo) decide where to plant their new fields and set out to clear a site, they look and listen for omens. They employ bird augury, a form of divination in which the calls and flight patterns of certain birds reveal messages from benevolent deities. The way the omens are interpreted encourages farmers to diversify and randomize their choices rather than making flawed assumptions based on last year's conditions (Dove 1993).

RECOMMENDED READING

Ann McElroy and Patricia K. Townsend. 2015. *Medical Anthropology in Ecological Perspective.* 6th ed. Boulder, CO: Westview Press. This introduction to the subdiscipline of medical anthropology from an environmental perspective expands the coverage of topics such as climate change, demography, food production, and infectious diseases.

Merrill Singer, ed. 2016. *A Companion to the Anthropology of Environmental Health.* Malden, MA: Wiley-Blackwell. A multi-authored reference volume on the political ecology of contemporary issues in environment and health edited by the anthropologist who originated the concept of syndemics.

RECOMMENDED FILM

Joe Berlinger et al. 2017. *From the Ashes.* 81 minutes. National Geographic Documentary Films. Environmental and health costs of coal mining in Appalachia and the American West.

Chapter Twelve

It Isn't Easy Being Green
Influencing
Environmental Policies

Anthropologists often find a challenge in being "green," that is, balancing personal and political engagement with environmental issues, scholarship that provides an understanding of those issues, the requirements of their employer or sponsoring agency, and their ethical commitments to the subjects of their research.

An environmental anthropologist is not always an environmental activist. An activist is motivated to work to protect the environment through political engagement and changes in personal consumption. Probably most environmental anthropologists would not choose to specialize in that area of study if we were not environmentally concerned, but it is certainly possible, just as researchers may study religion or marriage without themselves being believers or married people. Environmental anthropologists may differ in the degree of priority they give to the needs of people when they come into conflict with the needs of other species.

Ecological anthropologists who did fieldwork in the past most often studied the adaptation of human communities to their biotic and physical environment. Ecological anthropologists who do fieldwork now are just as likely to go to the offices of an environmental organization to observe and interview staff and volunteers. Even in a tropical village setting, rather than weighing sweet potatoes and measuring gardens, they are as likely to attend a meeting of villagers who are deciding how to manage their forest resources in response to an offer to sell logs to a timber company. Increasingly, ecological anthropologists seek employment as practicing anthropologists, working for institutions and organizations concerned with the environment. Persons with degrees in anthropology are hired to do full-time work that does not have the job title "anthropologist," but they use their social science skills on the job as administrators or project evaluators.

THE INDONESIAN FOREST FIRES OF 1997–1998

In 1998, Andrew Vayda traveled to Indonesia as a consultant to the World Wide Fund for Nature (WWF). Vayda was then a senior faculty member at Rutgers University who had many years earlier directed the project that took Roy Rappaport to New Guinea. Working alongside an Indonesian colleague, Ahmad Sahur, Vayda tried to explain the causes of the devastating forest fires that followed the drought of 1997–1998 (Vayda 1999). The burning of dry vegetation created a smoky haze that closed airports and caused respiratory problems all over Southeast Asia. Many of the fires were deliberately set to clear land for large agricultural projects that included a government-supported rice project and plantations of oil palms and other tree crops. Vayda and Sahur were interested in the cause of the remaining fires.

Government bureaucrats prefer to blame local farmers who use fires to clear land for cultivation as scapegoats for forest fires. Vayda could find no evidence that this was true. In areas under shifting cultivation, farmers were experienced in controlling fires for clearing land. A community must have sanctions to prevent people from damaging the fields and houses belonging to their neighbors.

Their fieldwork on the causes of fires led the researchers to look more closely at the illegal practice of cutting ironwood trees (*ulin*) for their strong, fire-resistant, durable wood. The ulin cutters used fire in several ways. They set fires to clear the underbrush to make it easier to cut and move the timber. They set campfires for their own comfort—to cook food, smoke cigarettes, and repel mosquitoes. Truckers, moving timber at night to evade the police, lit small fires if they had to stop to change a tire or take a break. Any of these fires could get out of control under the dry conditions. An underlying cause was that previous logging had left degraded forests more susceptible to burning than areas that had never been logged.

The illegal ironwood trade flourished because Indonesia was in an economic crisis with low wages and high unemployment. Because the trade was illegal, the researchers needed to use indirect methods to estimate its extent. They estimated the number of boatloads of timber that left the port nearest the forest. Then they calculated how many truckloads of trees would need to be cut down to fill these boats.

The research on forest fires was intended to form a solid basis for policy both on the part of the international environmental organization (WWF) and the Indonesian government. Obviously if either organization based its policies on the erroneous assumption that most fires were caused by village farmers clearing their fields, these policies would miss the mark badly.

ANIMAL RIGHTS IN THE NORTH

Following intense protests and boycotts, in 1983 the animal rights movement successfully achieved a ban on the import of sealskin into Europe's fashion market. The keystone of the campaign was a series of TV and magazine ads showing the slaughter of baby harp seals in Newfoundland. Even after this ban, the controversy continued, with protests at the time of the annual spring seal hunt and calls for new environmental regulations. In 2003, Canadian fisheries authorities increased seal-hunt quotas to cull a ballooning seal population and protect fisheries, touching off a new round of protests.

The antisealing campaigns failed to distinguish this commercial southern hunt from the aboriginal seal hunt of the far north. Nor did they make any distinction among the various species of seals. The European decision to ban sealskin imports did not rest on scientific study of the environmental issues that might allow a sustainable harvest of seals. The controversy was about animal rights versus human rights and only tangentially about the environment. The ban had a serious economic impact on the Canadian Inuit, for whom hunting, particularly of the ringed seal, continues to have importance.

To understand the northern seal controversy, an anthropologist needs to approach it from two angles: looking at the place of seal hunting in Inuit society and at the animal rights movement as a product of its cultural context in Europe and America. The "traditional" nature of Inuit hunting goes beyond the methods and economics of hunting; it is not a matter of technology, which has changed in the past few decades to incorporate outboard motors, snowmobiles, and rifles in place of skin boats, dog teams, and harpoons. Nor is it a matter of economics, for in addition to continuing to eat seal meat, the Inuit now require cash for ammunition, fuel, spare parts, and many other things. The traditional nature of the hunt lies in culture history, social relationships, and the relationship between people and animals. For the Inuit, encounters with animals are governed by moral relationships like those with humans. The social aspects of hunting are particularly important—who hunts with whom and how meat is shared. The Inuit have not ceased to be Inuit simply by being incorporated into the market economy (Wenzel 1991).

When anthropologists seek to advocate for the rights of indigenous people, as Wenzel did for the Inuit, it is not sufficient that they understand the indigenous people and their environment. The anthropologists also run up against their own culture's contradictory and paternalistic views of indigenous people (Brosius 1999). The Noble Savage view of the Inuit is that they are isolated people with superb survival strategies for meeting the challenge of an extreme environment and therefore deserving of paternalistic protection. If they are not that, then they must be fully modern and "just like us." Part of what anthropologists need to do is to picture the Inuit as "a traditional people living in the modern world," (Wenzel 1991:84) or as bicultural people who move between two worlds.

ENVIRONMENTAL MOVEMENTS

Whether environmentalism is expressed as individual concern or as an organized social movement, it is part of the culture in which it is found. Although there are international environmental organizations, environmentalism has unique forms and histories in different places, as in the United States and Germany, even though both are wealthy industrial countries. Environmental movements among rural people in low income countries take still different shapes. The political alliances that form between international environmental NGOs and indigenous minorities are often complex and fraught with mutual misunderstandings. One of the most useful things that anthropology can do is to study environmentalism itself and its expression in different cultures (Milton 1996).

The environmental movement has two major strands, "green" and "brown" environmentalism. The green movement is more concerned with conservation of the remaining wild places; the brown movement, more with cleaning up industrial pollution. Until recently, the major national conservation organizations had a largely green agenda and were not very interested in urban or industrial areas. A third strand, "white" environmentalism, can also be delineated. Its main concerns are the dangers posed by newer biotechnologies such as genetically modified food crops (Stone 2010). Each of these environmentalisms tends to draw its membership from among people occupying different strata of society as well as from people holding different values and ways of organizing.

PARKS AND PEOPLE

Frequently environmental anthropologists are engaged in the study of conservation conflicts. Such conflicts typically arise after government agencies and nongovernment organizations come into poor rural communities to create a national park or protected area. They promise benefits of economic development in exchange for land and labor. Often these benefits depend on the anticipated growth of ecotourism (West 2006, 2016). When the expected benefits do not materialize, disillusioned people who have lost land, livestock, or access to game animals face even more desperate poverty. As the remaining rural land becomes overpopulated, many of these "conservation refugees" migrate to the slums of urban areas without adequate means of supporting themselves.

How much land would need to be set aside as parks and other types of reserves to protect biological diversity fully? Biologist E. O.

Wilson (2016) suggests that it would require *half* of the Earth to be set aside for wildlife. As may well be imagined, creating such large reserves cuts deeply into lands already being used by people. Inevitably, those who are already poor and powerless are the ones who would lose the land they depend on.

Gorongosa National Park in Mozambique is one of the most influential examples of the problems and potentials of protected areas. In his publications, E. O. Wilson often draws on his travel to Gorongosa to illustrate his support for creating reserves, and the park has appeared in numerous television specials and glossy magazine articles. Gorongosa Park was a hunting reserve in Portuguese colonial days and officially became a national park in 1960, the government expelling its human residents in favor of tourists, lions, elephants, warthogs, and Cape buffalo. Gorongosa lost its place as a safari destination for international tourists when the post-Independence civil war heated up in the late 1970s. It was at the center of the country and the center of the conflict, during which the fighters decimated the animals and destroyed the infrastructure of the park. After the peace accords in 1992, large international conservation organizations became interested in restoring the park. Funding from a wealthy American, through the Carr Foundation, in collaboration with the Mozambiquan government, enabled aggressive work on the restoration to begin in 2008. According to the anthropologists following the project, intentions to involve local people in decision making quickly gave way to a top-down approach that expanded the boundaries of the park and ignored traditional land and water management, leading to new conflicts (Schuetze 2015; Walker 2015).

The term "fortress conservation" is the conservation strategy that sets aside protected areas such as national parks or game reserves and restricts local people from living, hunting, or herding there. The poorest countries generally have the most land set aside as protected areas; for example, Tanzania set aside almost one-third of its lands for conservation. The government decided that loss of traditional livelihoods by pastoralists was less significant that the expected income from tourism and the projects of international environmental organizations. Evidence was lacking that overgrazing had degraded all the designated land. To counter criticism of the injustice of dispossessing traditional users of the land, the large international environmental organizations presented "community conservation" as an alternative to fortress conservation. Local people were rewarded for managing their own resources sustainably. Anthropologists and geographers were enlisted to research the successes and failures of such conservation programs (Brockington 2002; Igoe 2004; West et al. 2006).

As is true for African game reserves, little was known about the ecology of the Calakmul Biosphere Reserve in Campeche, southern

Mexico, when it was created in 1989. It was set up on a largely political, rather than scientific, basis (Haenn 2005). Calakmul is Mexico's largest protected area for tropical ecosystems, containing threatened species such as tapir, jaguar, and ocelot, as well as encompassing the ruins of a large pre-Columbian Maya city. This area also had attracted migrants who fled nearby Chiapas in the 1980s to escape the Zapatista rebellion. To understand the political ecology of a protected area, one thus needs to consider the history, as well as the ecology, of the area.

Knowledge of the requirements of top predators such as the large cats is another necessity. Swedish ecologists studying snow leopards in Mongolia found that only a few of the protected areas across Asia were large enough to support a breeding population of snow leopards. In fact, nearly half of the protected areas were smaller than the range of a single adult male snow leopard. Conservationists realize that this demands that they work with communities in areas adjacent to parks (Johansson et al. 2016). Similarly, Project Tiger reserves in India require regional cooperation to mitigate tiger–human conflict. This work is made more challenging by the history of a state that disempowered local people (Read 2016). In tribal areas of India, where tribes have sometimes been uprooted from their ancestral lands to establish tiger reserves, belief in the sacredness of tigers made them appropriate stewards and candidates for comanagement projects.

RECOMMENDED READING

Susan Charnley and William H. Durham. 2010. "Anthropology and Environmental Policy: What Counts?" *American Anthropologist* 112(3): 397–415. Documenting a decline in quantitative and environmental data within environmental anthropology, the authors declare that reversing this trend is essential to increasing its policy relevance, using a Brazilian project and its impact on World Bank policy as a case study.

Nora Haenn and David G. Casagrande. 2007. "Citizens, Experts, and Anthropologists: Finding Paths in Environmental Policy." *Human Organization* 66(2): 99–102. Introduces a special issue of four papers on anthropologists' influence on creating and implementing environmental policy.

RECOMMENDED FILMS

Alethea Arnaquq-Baril, director. 2016. *Angry Inuk*. 85 minutes. EyeSteelFilm/ National Film Board of Canada. Defends the Inuit seal hunt in the filmmaker's home community of Kimmirut and follows several Inuit to Europe in their effort to have the ban on seal products overturned.

Jessica Yu, director. 2013. *The Guide*. 40 minutes. A teenager from Gorongosa dreams of becoming a tour guide until he shadows biologist E. O. Wilson collecting ants on his first visit to the park and gets hooked on science.

Also, several short videos of biological research on the website of the E. O. Wilson Biodiversity Laboratory https://eowilsonfoundation.org/gorongosa-field-notes/

Yung Chang, director. 2008. *Up the Yangtze*. 90 minutes. EyeSteelFilm/National Film Board of Canada/PBS/POV. Social dislocation caused by the building of China's Three Gorges Dam.

Chapter Thirteen

Holy Ground

F or the Yuin clans, Aborigines living in New South Wales, Australia, the mountain called Gulaga is the center of the world, the birthplace of the Yuin people, as well as a source of food and medicines. Yuin elders worked with anthropologists to record their traditions (Rose et al. 2003). The elders emphasized the sacredness of places on the mountain, comparing the rocks to a cathedral, only even more powerful and blessed, a place to sit and meditate. Mount Gulaga and nearby mountains are rounded outcrops and boulders of granite pushed up by ancient volcanoes. The Yuin had the mountain and surrounding eucalypt forest returned to their ownership as a National Park, which they comanage with the New South Wales Government. The sacred mountain is an example of an ancient conservation practice found around the world, the practice of recognizing certain landscapes as sacred places worthy of special respect.

On Mount Horeb (also called Mount Sinai), according to the third chapter of Exodus, the angel of Yahweh spoke to Moses from a burning bush, saying, "Take off your shoes, for the place on which you stand is holy ground." I chose the term "holy" in the title of this chapter to avoid choosing between the terms "sacred ecology" and "spiritual ecology," each of which have distinguished advocates (Berkes 1999; Sponsel 2012). What is sacred is simply what matters most to people, what they value most highly (Milton 2002). The valuation placed on environmental protection in any culture is not only a matter of rational self-interest and economic calculation but also of emotional attachments and ethical commitments, as E. N. Anderson argued in his book, *Ecologies of the Heart* (Anderson 1996).

"The Holy" or "spiritual" are broad enough terms to include both personal religion and organized religion. When people say, as many in highly individualistic modern societies do, "I consider myself spiritual but not religious," they usually mean that they are not committed to a religious community; that is, their religion is personal and not institutionalized. Experiences of the holy include religious experiences that are primarily emotional, that is, experiences of the numinous or mysterious, as well as those aspects of religion that are verbalized— ethics, creeds, and statements taken as God's commandments. All these aspects of religion, personal and institutional, emotional and rational, may be relevant to human adaptation to the environment (Rappaport 1999).

From Mount Sinai in the Middle East to Mount Gulaga in Australia to Devil's Tower in Wyoming, people indigenous to an area have identified mountain peaks as sacred places. Unusual phenomena such as whirlpools or oddly shaped rocks have also received this designation, as have rather ordinary-appearing bodies of water or stretches of country that are associated with significant shared memories.

Virtually the entire land area traditionally used by indigenous people may be suffused with sacred meaning. Anthropologists working with the U.S. Department of Energy consulted with the Indian tribes of Nevada regarding the cultural impacts of the transportation of radioactive wastes through their lands. The elders shared their concerns about "angry rock," their term for uranium ore, a substance known from archaeological sites in the area dating back thousands of years. The kinds of places with significance for spiritual well-being for the tribes greatly outnumbered the places with mere subsistence survival value. They included places where songs, visions, rituals, storytelling, and healing had taken place, as well as the sources of ritual substances such as paint, clay, and feathers (Stoffle and Arnold 2003).

Similarly, protesters in 2016 at Standing Rock opposed the Keystone XL oil pipeline that would cross the Missouri River, threatening the water supply of the nearby Lakota reservation. While they identified themselves as "Water Protectors," concerned about pollution of drinking water, and expressed specific concerns about Indian burial grounds for which informed consent had not been given, they also shared a more general respect for lands full of traditional meaning.

SACRED GROVES

It is not only ageless geological features of landscape such as mountains, caves, and rivers that may be deemed sacred by indigenous people but also living things such as trees. The existence of sacred groves is documented from widely different cultures and may be the oldest form of protecting biodiversity. Probably the best-known sacred groves are those protected by Buddhist monks in Thailand. Some of these are relatively small stands of trees surrounding temples, others are large tracts of forest, perhaps covering a whole mountaintop where a shrine has been built (Sponsel and Natadecha-Sponsel 2003). The Buddha was associated with trees at his birth, his enlightenment, and his passing (Darlington 2012:2).

Monks who are environmental activists began to ordain trees in the 1980s, wrapping them with the orange cloth of a Buddhist monk's robe, thereby consecrating the trees and calling attention to the threat of deforestation. This new form of engaged Buddhism was a response to the suffering of the rural poor as the clear-cutting of forests led to flooding and environmental degradation for timber and for monocrop plantations. Even the oldest of the world religions are living traditions that respond to socio-ecological change.

Though it is a planted food crop, a grove of cacao trees in parts of Central America is another kind of sacred grove. For the Maya of eastern Guatemala cacao and maize have been important ritual food plants since at least 600 B.C.E. The individual cacao tree itself is symbolic of a human being (like other upright trees bearing large fruits reminiscence of a human head). A chocolate drink containing ground maize is drunk as part of rain rituals and other ceremonies even today. It has been suggested that the fact that cacao trees grow in the shade of forest trees may have been an important incentive that protected the forests from excessive clearing by the Maya to expand maize farming beyond sustainable levels (Kufer, Grube, and Heinrich 2006).

In the Zambezi valley of Zimbabwe, in southern Africa, the amount of forest loss is dramatically less in forests that are now or were in the past considered to be sacred. Researchers determined this through interviews and community meetings in combination with aerial photographs that had been taken over a period of 33 years (Byers et al. 2001). The Zambezi sacred forests were dry forests growing on deep, sandy soils that were used as burial grounds. It was thought that the dense, thorny acacia trees might deter witches from using the corpses for evil purposes.

CREE HUNTERS

For the 5,000 years since the retreat of the glaciers, the Northern Algonquian group known as the James Bay Cree have lived in the boreal forest of the subarctic region southeast of Hudson Bay and James Bay, Canada. Other groups of Cree are found across Canada from Labrador to Alberta. The environmental relationships of contemporary Cree hunters are among the most thoroughly studied indigenous systems of knowledge related to subsistence (Feit 2004).

For three centuries after contact with Euro-Canadian fur traders, the St. James Cree lived primarily by hunting, trapping, and fishing, finally settling in the 1960s into nine larger permanent communities in Quebec that are in more regular contact with outposts of the dominant industrial society. The construction of the James Bay hydroelectric project in the 1970s increased the intensity of those contacts, as did increased harvesting of the forests for timber. Many of them continue hunting and fishing for subsistence, even while living an otherwise modern existence that includes purchasing food in stores.

In the worldview of the Cree hunter, humans do not control the hunt. The fish and game are not there simply to be taken. Rather it is the animals who control the success of the hunt by offering themselves willingly to people (or, conversely, choosing to withhold themselves from a hunter). The Cree credit animals with knowing the same things that people know and being able to communicate and share that knowledge with people (Berkes 1999:80). Humans and animals are in a relationship of reciprocity, just as humans are in a relationship with other humans. Indeed, anthropologists argue more generally that in all cultures, including those that are modern and postmodern, there are profound connections between the ways that people engage with each other and with other species (Hornborg 2003).

To have hunting success, the Cree assert, one must show respect to animals, maintaining an attitude of humility rather than boasting. A respectful hunter will follow rules that signify respect when he kills, carries, butchers, and consumes meat and disposes of the bones and inedible remains of the hunt. Nothing should be wasted; therefore, purely recreational or sport hunting with no intention of eating the meat is inappropriate. Noise and mess are to be avoided. Offerings to the animal can be made with tobacco or by throwing pieces of the meat into the fire (Berkes 1999:83–87).

A system of hunting territories regulates Cree hunting, each under the stewardship of elders called "tallyman" or "steward." The stewards usually inherit their positions and name their successors from among hunters who have grown up knowing the territory. The approximately 300 territories range in size from about 300 to several thousand square kilometers. By consulting among themselves about their experiences, the elders can make decisions about which areas to hunt or fish intensively. Other hunting areas or fishing lakes are left to rest for a few years to allow wildlife populations to recover.

Several research studies have indicated that the Cree system of adaptive management does work to maintain sustainable harvests of moose, beaver, fish, and geese. Does this mean that Cree never make mistakes in managing wildlife? Certainly not. Chisasibi Cree elders report that when their ancestors first got repeating rifles in 1910, they killed caribou wastefully and without respect. They believed that this violation of the hunting ethic is the reason that caribou disappeared from the Chisasibi area until the winter of 1982–1983. The story of the disaster of 1910 was retained in oral history through generations and informed the way that this group hunted the caribou when they finally returned (Berkes 1999:101–106).

THE GANGES RIVER:
RAW SEWAGE OR SPIRITUAL POWER

While anthropologists have gained a reputation as students of the traditional religions practiced by Native Americans and other indigenous peoples, they have not neglected studying adherents of the three largest global religions: Christianity, Islam, and Hinduism. Seventy percent of the people of the world are adherents of those three global religions: 2.3 billion Christians, and 1.8 billion Muslims, and 1.1 billion Hindus (Pew Research Institute 2017). Each of the global religions has theological, moral, and ethical principles that support respect for creation. Whatever the similarities and differences in their ecotheology, followers of all the global religions have generally fallen short when they came to put their own environmental teachings into practice.

Anthropologists of religion, along with philosophers and theologians, engage in cross-cultural comparisons of these environmental theologies of world religions (UNEP 1999). Ethnographers especially study the interplay of belief and practice at the local level. One such research project is the work of anthropologist Kelly Alley on the sacred river of India, the Ganges (Ganga).

The Ganga River flows 2,500 km from the Himalayas of northern India towards the south and west and flows through Bangladesh and into the Bay of Bengal. Along the way, it drains one quarter of India's geographic area and is diverted for irrigated agriculture and drinking water for as many as 500 million people living in cities and towns along the riverbank. These settlements and the industries in them dump their sewage, much of it untreated, into the river. Alley's multisite fieldwork took her to Banaras (officially called Varanasi) and the other large cities in Uttar Pradesh, India's most heavily industrialized state. The industries here include the processing of sugar and other foods, leather, textiles, pulp and paper, and chemicals. Wastewater treatment has not kept pace with the growth of population and industry; the river is highly contaminated with toxic chemicals, fecal coliform bacteria, and other pollutants. Plastic bags of garbage float in the river. Cremated and partially cremated corpses are ritually disposed of in the river.

Clearly the water of the Ganges is dirty, in the hygienic sense, but this does not necessarily mean that it is ritually polluted. Many anthropologists have pointed out that the categories of physical cleanliness and ritual purity are not identical. Priests and pilgrims may acknowledge that the water is disgustingly dirty and still insist that the goddess Ganga is known from the sacred texts of Hinduism to possess the power of spiritual purification and renewal of the cosmos. Many people bathe in the sacred water of the Ganges daily and millions more make pilgrimages to bathe in it annually. Temples and shrines are located at many sites from the headwaters to far downstream. With individual exceptions, Hindu religious belief has not yet served to motivate modern environmental activism, Alley asserts, because it sees the river as an all-forgiving Mother (Alley 2002).

ENVIRONMENTAL JUSTICE IN THE UNITED STATES

Within all the global religions, different theological strands may welcome or reject environmental concerns. Within Hinduism, this manifests itself in differences between those who emphasize the transcendence or immanence of the goddess. There are parallel theological strands within Christianity, differences between those who emphasize God as transcendent and separate from creation, and those who emphasize the incarnation (God taking on human flesh in Jesus Christ) and God's intention to redeem the whole of a fallen creation.

Christians also differ in eschatology, that is, their view of the last things. At one extreme are those who consider care for the Earth as foolish, with the Rapture and End Times soon to come. They are poles apart from those who regard care for Creation as a measure of their respect for the Creator and their love for and duty to future generations.

Despite these theological differences, there is no doubt that, especially in the United States, organized religious groups have played a significant role in social movements pressing for the identification and cleanup of toxic, industrially polluted sites. Usually this involvement has derived less from their theology of the environment than from their concern for injustice suffered by their human neighbors.

My first awareness of (and involvement in) this social movement came at a meeting that I attended at a Methodist church in the Love Canal neighborhood of Niagara Falls, New York, in 1979. During the previous year, neighborhood residents, led by Lois Gibbs, a young housewife and mother, had begun actively protesting the danger they perceived from the building of their homes and elementary school on top of a former waste dump site for the local chemical industry. Folks from many churches throughout western New York came together at the church to organize a group called the Ecumenical Task Force on Love Canal. Its ministry of relief and advocacy for the residents of the neighborhood, and later for neighbors of other toxic sites, was modeled on the help that these churches had traditionally offered during so-called "natural" disasters. It led to the recognition of a new kind of disaster, the technological or toxic disaster.

Ultimately the residents closest to Love Canal were relocated to other neighborhoods. The school and many homes were razed. The site was cleaned up under the newly designed federal Superfund program, whose very existence was in large part due to activism at Love Canal.

Greater awareness of toxic wastes led to protesting the sites of proposed landfills. One such protest in 1982 took place in predominantly African American rural Warren County, North Carolina, which was proposed as a disposal site for polychlorinated biphenyl (PCB). Support for this protest brought together the existing environmental and civil rights movements into a new movement for environmental justice. It took further inspiration from a 1987 study by the United Church of Christ, *Toxic Wastes and Race in the United States*, that showed the relationship of toxic sites to income and ethnicity. The environmental justice movement incorporates church and community groups, drawn together by shared concern for the unjust burden of exposure to toxic wastes on people of color, tribal members, and the poor (Lee 2002).

One example of the environmental justice movement is the Hyde Park neighborhood of Augusta, Georgia. African American homeowners there learned in 1991 that their garden produce and soil were contaminated with arsenic and chromium. Nine polluting industrial sites surrounding their homes included wood-preserving and paper plants and a junkyard. Multiple environmental studies produced conflicting results as to the nature and seriousness of the threats to human health. Seeking redress and relocation away from the contamination, neighborhood volunteers formed HAPIC (the Hyde and Aragon Park Improvement Committee) to work actively for environmental justice. The leader of HAPIC, the Rev. Charles Utley, was a minister, as are the leaders of many other environmental justice organizations in African American communities (Checker 2005).

RECOMMENDED READING

Barbara R Johnston, ed. 2011. *Life and Death Matters: Human Rights, Environment, and Social Justice*. New York, Left Coast Press. Anthropologists examine environmental justice issues of economic development, conservation, mines, conflict, and climate change.

Eugene N. Anderson. 1996. *Ecologies of the Heart: Emotion, Belief, and the Environment*. New York: Oxford University Press. From his fieldwork among Chinese fishermen in Hong Kong, Maya farmers in Mexico, and elsewhere, Anderson demonstrates that when traditional peoples have managed their resources well they have done so with the support of powerful cultural symbols engaging emotion and religion.

Leslie E Sponsel. 2012. *Spiritual Ecology: A Quiet Revolution*. Santa Barbara, CA: Praeger/ ABC-CLIO, LLC. Sponsel is the leading anthropological spokesperson for spiritual ecology as the cross-cultural approach that bridges global religion, ethics, social action, and personal experience in environmentalism.

RECOMMENDED FILMS

Christopher McCleod, producer/director. 2001. *In the Light of Reverence*. 72 minutes. Earth Island Institute. Three sites sacred to the Wintu, Lakota, and Hopi: Mt. Shasta, Devil's Tower, and the Colorado Plateau.

Christopher McCleod, producer/director. 2013. *Standing on Sacred Ground*. 4 films, 55 minutes each. Earth Island Institute/Bullfrog Films. A documentary film series exploring threats to places of spiritual significance in another eight indigenous cultures.

Chapter Fourteen

Consumer Cultures

When we first returned to the United States from fieldwork in Papua New Guinea, we experienced *reverse culture shock*. At first I kept asking, "Why is everyone all dressed up in their good clothes? Is something special happening?" My husband, Bill, was overwhelmed by the size of the supermarket and the huge number of product choices. After we made these initial adjustments to a home culture where we no longer seemed entirely at home, deeper questions remained. One of these is, "Can the Saniyo teach us anything about how to live sustainably?"

Some ecological anthropologists say yes. They are confident that human systems of knowledge and action that are ecologically sensitive can evolve in the future. Studies of very different ways of life such as that of the Culina of Peru or the Saniyo-Hiyowe of Papua New Guinea contribute to our understanding of the evolutionary or adaptive processes that lead to sustainability and will contribute to this goal.

Other anthropologists say no, forest peoples have little to teach us. Modern life is different in principle, and there is no going back. Dominated by market forces, we now see nature as an impersonal source of resources and services. We no longer see nature as a personal being or beings with whom we might be in relationship. Nature is "it," not "thou."

My own sense is that neither of these is quite true: I am not optimistic about our ability, as a species, to learn to live sustainably before irreversible damage is done to the biosphere—damage of a magnitude sufficient to lead to our own extinction as a species. Even so, pessimism does not get us off the hook as individuals, families, and communities to do our best to change this. Such change may require us to change our own lifestyle and to advocate for change in policies in our local community and our nation. Along these lines, it seems to me that the most important thing the Saniyo can teach us is to recognize the *abnormality* of our high-consumption way of life. By experiencing other cultures, even in books or film, I am hopeful that we may be able to keep alive a sense of "reverse culture shock." In other words, we may become more aware of the size of our *ecological footprint*.

ECOLOGICAL FOOTPRINT ANALYSIS

Anthropologists did not invent the concept of an ecological footprint, but it is consistent with the way that ecological anthropologists compare the *carrying capacity* of lands under different systems of food production. In addition to land used for food production, the *ecological footprint* includes land needed for forest products and the disposal of wastes to estimate the total load on the ecosphere (Wackernagel and Rees 1996). The footprint concept is related to what Swedish anthropologist Alf Hornborg calls the "environmental load displacement" that began with the Industrial Revolution. It is an unequal exchange between the industrialized regions and the extractive regions that provide raw materials and fuels. Hornborg views most modern technology as a social means of displacing work and environmental degradation to areas where labor, land, and damage to the environment cost less (Hornborg 2016:35).

The ecological footprint of the average North American living in the United States measures 8.6 hectares (21.3 acres). The average footprint of a person in India is substantially less at 1.1 hectares (2.7 acres) (Global Footprint Network 2003–2017). Even so, the total for India is more than the total area of India's productive land. How can this be? It means that India's economy is not sustainable. India is a net importer of food and is depleting its natural capital by cutting its forests.

Industrial nations are consuming much more than their ecologically productive area can produce. They also meet this deficit by importing resources and depleting natural capital. Today's globalized economy is not sustainable. Humanity's ecological footprint exceeds global biocapacity and is growing faster than nature can regenerate, risking ecological collapse unless patterns of consumption are altered. The intensity of human use of the planet is due to the increasing scale of operations of the economy as well as to population growth. Another doubling of the world population, which is likely to occur in our lifetime, will exceed many of the resources available to support human life.

EUROPEAN AND AMERICAN CONSUMERS

A cultural anthropologist does not have to go as far as Papua New Guinea to observe differences in consumption and lifestyle. Ethnography of small towns in Minnesota and Sweden showed that the two towns were similar, in that both belong to industrial consumer societies. Although they may express disgust at materialism and consumerism, each town's residents carry on acquiring more. Status symbols in both communities included vehicles, label clothing, and electronics. Americans favored big homes in new developments while Swedes emphasized impressive yards and high-quality home furnishings (Erickson 1997).

Nationally the Swedes used only 70 to 80 percent per person of what Americans used, enough to make a difference in their contribution to global environmental problems, but the pattern of use differed. Swedes used more heating fuel, keeping their thermostats up at night and ventilating the house by opening windows and doors. The Americans made more use of appliances; watched more TV; and owned more air conditioners, humidifiers, and clothes driers. In other environmental behaviors, the two communities differed, too. Minnesota was a leading state in recycling in the United States, but the residents of the Swedish town were far more involved in recycling glass and paper. The Swedish families were more likely to compost yard or kitchen waste and less likely to use pesticides, which are strictly regulated in Sweden.

Anthropology is particularly well suited to study the cultural basis of preferences for consumer goods. There had not been a great deal of research on this aspect of material culture in modern society until British social anthropologist Daniel Miller and his students began looking at people's "stuff"—everyday things like blue jeans— and going shopping with them. In one ethnographic study, they spent 17 months visiting households on a street in London, producing an account of how people used their possessions to express themselves and their relationships. Some collected music CDs or tattoos, some kept photographs or old toys, while a few had relatively bare living spaces (Miller 2008).

Consumer goods are embodied energy. They represent the use of energy in manufacturing, distribution, and disposal. All of these processes burden the environment. It has been estimated that it would take at least three planets for everyone now living on Earth to live like this (Wackernagel and Rees 1996:15).

After studying the concept of ecological footprint and global environmental change, many thoughtful people conclude that they need to reduce their personal consumption. Josiah Heyman notes that this leads his students to alternate between "greed and guilt," between wanting more "stuff" and anxiety about having too much. This frustration reveals that they may be thinking too narrowly about consumption. Only a small part of consumption is the result of conscious, personal choices such as buying a hamburger or a pair of running shoes. The larger consumption issues, such as energy sources, housing, and transportation systems, are not made on the individual level. Developing theories that will lead to good policy choices needs to be done by thinking on multiple levels of analysis—individual, household, community, nation, and multinational corporation (Heyman 2004; Wilk 2002).

RECOMMENDED READING

WWF. 2016. *The Living Planet Report 2016: Risk and Resilience in a New Era*. Gland, Switzerland: WWF International. The most recent of annual reports that reflect the ecological footprint of human population and consumption. http://www.footprintnetwork.org/content/documents/2016_ Living_Planet_Report_Lo.pdf

RECOMMENDED FILMS

Linda Booker, director. 2017. *Straws*. 33 minutes. Video Project. Plastic straws, though recently invented to replace sustainable alternatives, quickly became one of the top items of beach pollution and washed into oceans.

Annie Leonard, writer/narrator. 2007. *The Story of Stuff*. 20 minutes. Quick look at the environmental and social costs of our production and consumption patterns. Download animated film and annotated and referenced script at http://www.storyofstuff.com. This popular film was followed by similar short animated films at the website that deal with other aspects of sustainable living.

Daniel B. Gold and Judith Helfand, directors. 2002. *Blue Vinyl*. 98 minutes. Bullfrog Films. Helfand's quest to replace the vinyl siding on her parents' home after learning of the dangers of manufacturing and using polyvinyl chloride.

Glossary

Adaptation. A process of change or adjustment that is beneficial for a population, making individual organisms more suited to the stresses of their environment.

Agriculture. Farming of an intensive type using irrigation or terracing and plows drawn by animals or tractors.

Anthropogenic. Caused by humans.

Anthropocene. The geological epoch dating from the commencement of significant human impact on the Earth's geology and ecosystems. The Anthropocene Working Group proposed its adoption to the International Geological Congress in 2016, but it has not yet been ratified by the parent groups.

Applied anthropology. The use of anthropology to solve practical problems.

Aquifer. An underground layer of porous rock or sediment that contains the water that supplies wells and springs.

Archaeology. The subfield of anthropology that studies the material remains of people of the past.

Bacteria. Single-celled microorganisms that have a cell wall (unlike viruses) but lack a nucleus. Many are harmless, but others cause infectious diseases.

Bioarchaeologist. The specialist studying the human skeletal material found at archaeological sites, using the same skills that a forensic anthropologist uses with evidence of a crime or accident.

Biodiversity. The variety of life, including the full range of variation in species, ecosystems, populations, and genes.

Biological anthropology. The subfield of anthropology that studies the physical (biological) aspects of the human species.

Carrying capacity. The size of population that can be supported by an area of land.

Caste. A hereditary social group associated with an occupation in a hierarchy of such groups.

Circumscribed. Enclosed or surrounded, often by a geographical barrier.

Cognitive. Having to do with perceiving and thinking.

Cultural anthropology. The subfield of anthropology that studies the ways of life of contemporary people.

Cultural ecology. A theoretical perspective that emphasizes the importance of the natural environment in shaping core features of culture, including technology and economics.

Cultural relativism. The principle that cultures are to be evaluated in terms of their own values and not those of another culture.

Culture. A way of life; all that people learn to do, say, make, and think as members of society.

Ecological anthropology. The study of relationships between a population of humans and their biophysical environment.

Ecological footprint. The area of land that would be required to support a defined human population at its current material standard of living indefinitely; a measure of the load placed on the environment by using resources and disposing of wastes.

Ecosystem. A system formed by interactions within a community of different species of organisms, including humans, and its biophysical environment, characterized by flows of information, energy, and matter.

Emerging disease. A disease appearing for the first time in a population and increasing rapidly in incidence.

Environmental anthropology. The use of anthropology's methods and theories to contribute to the understanding of local or global environmental problems.

Equilibrium. Balance in a system, generally understood to be maintained by controlling fluctuations.

Ethnoecology. The study of the knowledge and beliefs about nature that are held in a culture, a broad cover term that includes such subdisciplines as ethnobotany, ethnozoology, and ethnobiology.

Feedback. A response that is used to alter a later response in a system, including *negative feedback*, which contributes to regulating the system, and *positive feedback*, which amplifies changes and leads to the collapse or transformation of the system.

Feral. Having escaped from domestication and become wild, as in feral pig.

Foraging. Subsistence from the wild through obtaining food by hunting and gathering.

Fossil aquifer Water source containing ancient water that is not renewable, either because it is now sealed off by an impermeable rock layer or the area no longer receives enough precipitation to recharge the aquifer.

Hacienda. (Spanish) A large ranch or farm owned by a member of the elite class.

Hazard. Something that causes danger or risk, especially of injury or death.

Historical ecology. The study of regional change in the landscape over time, drawing on the disciplines of anthropology, archaeology, geography, biology, and history.

Horticulture. Farming of a less intensive kind using hand tools. A long fallow period restores the land without need for irrigation or fertilizers.

Landscape. A mosaic of interacting ecosystems usually covering a fairly large area such as a watershed, but defined by a culture (or by a researcher looking from the perspective of another species).

Linguistics. The science of language. As a subfield of anthropology, anthropological linguistics is primarily concerned with systematically describing a language as a part of the culture in which it occurs.

Niche (ecological). A species' distinctive way of living, using resources, and relating to competitors, its specialized role in the environment.

Nongovernment organization (NGO). Voluntary organization such as charitable or environmental organization.

Optimal foraging model. A theory that predicts that humans and other predators will hunt the species that provide the best short-term return for their effort, regardless of cultural preferences or long-term effects.

Papua New Guinea. A country in the South Pacific that became independent from Australia in 1975. It occupies the eastern half of the island of New Guinea.

Political ecology. An orientation to research in environmental studies that espouses the viewpoint that relationships between humans and their environment cannot be understood without considering inequalities of power and wealth, especially those produced by the global economy.

Population. An interacting local group of individuals within which most mating takes place.

Resilience. The capacity of a system to absorb disturbances, change, and persist.

Reservoir. A population of animals that maintains a parasite or other pathogen from which humans may become infected.

Risk. The likelihood of some event, such as acquiring a disease or experiencing an accident.

Savanna. A tropical grassland environment.

Semantic domain. A set of terms in a language within an area of knowledge, such as a set of kinship terms or plant names.

Sustainability. The degree to which a given practice or material standard of living can continue without using up the ability to do so in the future.

Syndemic. A harmful interaction of two or more diseases or health conditions in a population, most often exacerbated by social and economic inequality.

System. A set of objects and their relationships.

Systems theory. A set of analogies drawn from computers and electronics and applied to biology, ecology, and other fields to understand communication and the flow of energy and information. Such cybernetic models differ from simple mechanical models by incorporating *feedback*.

Vector. An insect that is a carrier of a disease organism.

Virus. A microorganism consisting of nucleic acid in a protein capsule that can grow and replicate itself only within other cells. The infective agent in many emerging diseases.

World system. The largest unit in which economy and politics make sense. In past times equivalent to an empire (e.g. the Roman empire, Han China) but since the nineteenth century generally seen as the global capitalist world system. The best-known proponent of this concept is Immanuel Wallerstein. It is influential in environmental history and political ecology.

References

Alley, Kelly D. 2002. *On the Banks of the Ganga: When Wastewater Meets a Sacred River.* Ann Arbor: University of Michigan Press.

Almendares, J. et al. 1993. "Critical Regions, a Profile of Honduras." *Lancet* 342(8884): 1400–1402.

Alvard, Michael. 1995. "Intraspecific Prey Choice by Amazonian Hunters." *Current Anthropology* 36(5): 789–818.

Anderson, Eugene N. 1996. *Ecologies of the Heart: Emotion, Belief, and the Environment.* New York: Oxford University Press.

Andrews, E. Wyllys, and William Leonard Fash, eds. 2005. *Copán: The History of an Ancient Maya Kingdom.* Santa Fe, NM: School of American Research.

Balée, William. 1999. "Mode of Production and Ethnobotanical Vocabulary: A Controlled Comparison of Guajá and Ka'apor." In *Ethnoecology: Knowledge, Resources, and Rights,* ed. T. L. Gragson and B. G. Blount, pp. 24–40. Athens: University of Georgia Press.

Balée, William L., and Clark L. Erickson. 2006. *Time and Complexity in Historical Ecology: Studies in the Neotropical Lowlands.* New York: Columbia University Press.

Barth, Fredrik. 1956. "Ecological Relationships of Ethnic Groups in Swat, North Pakistan." *American Anthropologist* 58:1079–1089.

———. 2007. "Overview: Sixty Years in Anthropology." *Annual Review of Anthropology* 36: 1–16.

Berkes, Fikret. 1999. *Sacred Ecology: Traditional Ecological Knowledge and Resource Management.* Philadelphia, PA: Taylor & Francis.

Biersack, Aletta, and James B. Greenberg, eds. 2006. *Reimagining Political Ecology.* Durham, NC: Duke University Press.

Blaikie, Piers M. 1994. *At Risk: Natural Hazards, People's Vulnerability, and Disasters.* London: Routledge. (Second Edition. 2004. Ben Wisner, ed.)

Bolin, Inge. 2009. "The Glaciers of the Andes are Melting: Indigenous and Anthropological Knowledge Merge in Restoring Water Resources." In *Anthropology and Climate Change: From Encounters to Actions,* ed. Susan A. Crate and Mark Nuttall, pp. 228–239. Abingdon, UK: Taylor & Francis.

Bolten, Catherine E. 2016. "Circulating Ebola in the Anthropocene." *Anthropology News* 57(7): e89–e91. doi: 0.1111/AN.48.

Brauer, Jurgen. 2009. *War and Nature: The Environmental Consequences of War in a Globalized World.* Lanham MD: AltaMira Press.

Bridge, Gavin. 2004. "Contested Terrain: Mining and the Environment." *Annual Review of Environment & Resources* 29(1): 205–259.

Brockington, Dan. 2002. *Fortress Conservation: The Preservation of the Mkomazi Game Reserve Tanzania.* Bloomington: Indiana University Press.

Brosius, J. Peter. 1999. "Analyses and Interventions: Anthropological Engagements with Environmentalism." *Current Anthropology* 40(3): 277–309.

———. 2006. "What Counts as Local Knowledge in Global Environmental Assessments and Conventions?" In *Bridging Scales and Knowledge Systems,* ed. W. V. Reid, F. Berkes, T. J. Wilbanks, and D. Capistrano, pp. 129–144. Washington, DC: Island Press.

Button, Gregory V. 1995. "What You Don't Know Can't Hurt You: The Right to Know and the Shetland Island Oil Spill." *Human Ecology* 23(2): 241–258.

———. 2010. *Disaster Culture: Knowledge and Uncertainty in the Wake of Human and Environmental Catastrophe.* Walnut Creek, CA: Left Coast Press.

Byers, Bruce A., Robert N. Cunliffe, and Andrew T. Hudak. 2001. "Linking the Conservation of Culture and Nature: A Case Study of Sacred Forests in Zimbabwe." *Human Ecology* 29(2):187–218.

Cachelin, A., R. Norvell, and A. Darling. 2010. "Language Fouls in Teaching Ecology: Why Traditional Metaphors Undermine Conservation Literacy." *Conservation Biology* 24(3): 669–674.

Cannon, Terry. 2002. "Gender and Climate Hazards in Bangladesh." *Gender & Development* 10(2): 45–50.

Carneiro, Robert L. 1970. "A Theory of the Origin of the State." *Science* 169: 733–738.

Carson, Rachel. 1962. *Silent Spring.* Boston: Houghton Mifflin.

Cellarius, Barbara A. 2004. *In the Land of Orpheus: Rural Livelihoods and Nature Conservation in Postsocialist Bulgaria.* Madison: University of Wisconsin Press.

Chambers, Keith, and Anne Chambers. 2001. *Unity of Heart: Culture and Change in a Polynesian Atoll Society.* Long Grove, IL: Waveland Press.

Checker, Melissa. 2005. *Polluted Promises: Environmental Racism and the Search for Justice in a Southern Town.* New York: New York University Press.

Cole, John W., and Eric R. Wolf. 1974. *The Hidden Frontier: Ecology and Ethnicity in an Alpine Valley.* New York: Academic Press.

Conklin, Harold C. 1954 "An Ethnoecological Approach to Shifting Agriculture." New York Academy of Sciences, *Transactions Series* 2(17): 133–142.

Crumley, Carole L. 1993. *Historical Ecology: Cultural Knowledge and Changing Landscapes.* Santa Fe, NM: School of American Research Press.

———, ed. 2001. *New Directions in Anthropology & Environment: Intersections.* Walnut Creek, CA: AltaMira.

Darlington, Susan M. 2012. *Ordination of a Tree: The Thai Buddhist Environmental Movement.* Albany: State University of New York Press.

Davis, Reade. 2014. "A Cod Forsaken Place? Fishing in an Altered State in Newfoundland." *Anthropological Quarterly* 87(3): 695–726.

Descola, Philippe. 1994. *In the Society of Nature: A Native Ecology in Amazonia*. Cambridge, U.K.; New York; Paris: Cambridge University Press; Editions de la Maison des sciences de l'homme.

———. 1996. *The Spears of Twilight: Life and Death in the Amazon Jungle*. New York: New Press.

Donovan, D. G., and R. K. Puri. 2004. "Learning from Traditional Knowledge of Non-timber Forest Products: Penan Benalui and the Autecology of *Aquilaria* in Indonesian Borneo." *Ecology and Society* (3). http://www.ecologyandsociety.org/vol9/iss3/art3/

Dove, Michael R. 1993. "Uncertainty, Humility, and Adaptation in the Tropical Forest: The Agricultural Augury of the Kantu'." *Ethnology* 32(2): 145–168.

Durham, William H. 1995. "Political Ecology and Environmental Destruction in Latin America." In *The Social Causes of Environmental Destruction in Latin America*, ed. M. Painter and W. H. Durham, pp. 249–264. Ann Arbor: University of Michigan Press.

Early, John D., and Thomas N. Headland. 1998. *Population Dynamics of a Philippine Rain Forest People: The San Ildefonso Agta*. Gainesville: University Press of Florida.

Ehrlich, Paul R., and Anne H. Ehrlich. 1990. *The Population Explosion*. New York: Simon and Schuster.

Erickson, Rita J. 1997. *"Paper or Plastic?" Energy, Environment, and Consumerism in Sweden and America*. Westport, CT: Praeger.

Escobar, Arturo. 1998. "Constructing Nature: Elements for a Poststructural Political Ecology." In *Liberation Ecologies: Environment, Development, Social Movements*, ed. R. Peet and M. Watts, pp. 46–68. London: Routledge.

Farmer, Paul. 2004. "An Anthropology of Structural Violence." *Current Anthropology* 45(3): 305–325

Feit, Harvey A. 2004. "James Bay Cree's Life Projects and Politics: Histories of Place, Animal Partners and Enduring Relationships." In *In the Way of Development: Indigenous Peoples, Life Projects, and Globalization*, ed. M. Blaser, H. A. Feit, and G. McRae, pp. 97–116. London: Zed Books in association with Canadian International Development Research Centre, Ottawa.

Fox, Deane Niblack. 2016. "Agent Orange: Toxic Chemical, Narrative of Suffering, Metaphor for War." In *Looking Back on the Vietnam War: Twenty-first-Century Perspectives*, ed. Brenda M. Boyle and Jeehyun Lim, pp. 140–155. New Brunswick, NJ: Rutgers University Press.

Fratkin, Elliot M. 2004. *Ariaal Pastoralists of Kenya: Surviving Drought and Development in Africa's Arid Lands*. 2nd ed. (Cultural Survival Studies in Ethnicity and Change) Boston: Allyn & Bacon.

Frey, Rodney. 2001. *Landscape Traveled by Coyote and Crane: The World of the* Schitsu'umsh (Coeur d'Alene Indians). Seattle: University of Washington Press.

Geertz, Clifford. 1963. *Agricultural Involution*. Berkeley: Published for the Association of Asian Studies by University of California Press.

Global Footprint Network. 2003–2017. "Ecological Footprint." http://www.footprintnetwork.org/our-work/ecological-footprint/

Golson, Jack et al., eds. 2017. Ten Thousand Years of Cultivation at Kuk Swamp in the Highlands of Papua New Guinea (Terra Australis 46). Canberra: ANU Press.

Haenn, Nora. 2005. *Fields of Power, Forests of Discontent: Culture, Conservation, and the State in Mexico*. Tucson: University of Arizona Press.

Hardin, Rebecca, and Melissa J. Remis. 2006. "Biological and Cultural Anthropology of a Changing Tropical Forest: A Fruitful Collaboration across Subfields." *American Anthropologist* 108(2): 273–285.

Hassol, Susan. 2004. "Impacts of a Warming Arctic: Arctic Climate Impact Assessment." http://www.acia.uaf.edu

Hernández-Morcillo, Mónica, et al. 2014. "Traditional Ecological Knowledge in Europe: Status Quo and Insights for the Environmental Policy Agenda." *Environment* 56(1): 3–17. doi: 10.1080/00139157.2014.861673.

Heyman, Josiah McC. 2004. "The Political Ecology of Consumption: Beyond Greed and Guilt." In *Political Ecology across Spaces, Scales, and Social Groups*, ed. S. Paulson and L. L. Gezon, pp. 113–132. New Brunswick, NJ: Rutgers University Press.

Hill, Kim, and A. Magdalena Hurtado. 1996. *Aché Life History: The Ecology and Demography of a Foraging People*. New York: Aldine de Gruyter.

Hornborg, Alf. 2003. "From Animal Masters to Ecosystem Services: Exchange, Personhood, and Human Ecology." In *Imagining Nature: Practices of Cosmology and Identity*, ed. A. Roepstorff, N. Bubandt, and K. Kull, pp. 97–116. Aarhus, Denmark: University Press.

———. 2016. *Global Magic: Technologies of Appropriation from Ancient Rome to Wall Street*. New York: Palgrave Macmillan.

Hornborg, Alf, and Carole L. Crumley, eds. 2007. *The World System and the Earth System: Global Socioenvironmental Change and Sustainability since the Neolithic*. Walnut Creek, CA: Left Coast Press.

Hornborg, Alf, John McNeill, Robert Martínez, and Juan Alier, eds. 2007. *Rethinking Environmental History: World-System History and Global Environmental Change*. Lanham, MD: AltaMira Press.

Howell, Nancy. 1979. *Demography of the Dobe !Kung*. New York: Academic Press.

Hunn, Eugene. 1989. "Ethnoecology: The Relevance of Cognitive Anthropology for Human Ecology." In *The Relevance of Culture*, ed. M. Freilich, pp. 145–160. New York: Bergin & Garvey.

Hunn, Eugene S., and James Selam. 1990. *Nch'i-wána, "The Big River": Mid-Columbia Indians and Their Land*. Seattle: University of Washington Press.

Hunt, Terry L., and Carl P. Lipo. 2011. *The Statues that Walked: Unraveling the Mystery of Easter Island*. New York: Free Press.

Hurtado, A. Magdalena et al. 2003. "Longitudinal Study of Tuberculosis Outcomes among Immunologically Naive Aché Natives of Paraguay." *American Journal of Physical Anthropology* 121(2): 134–150.

Hyndman, David. 1994. *Ancestral Rain Forests & the Mountain of Gold: Indigenous Peoples and Mining in New Guinea*. Boulder, CO: Westview Press.

Igoe, Jim. 2004. *Conservation and Globalization: A Study of the National Parks and Indigenous Communities from East Africa to South Dakota*. Belmont, CA: Thomson/Wadsworth.

Johansson, Örjan et al. 2016. "Land Sharing Is Essential for Snow Leopard Conservation." *Biological Conservation* 203: 1–7.

Johnson, Leslie Main. 2010. *Trail of Story, Traveller's Path: Reflections on Ethnoecology and Landscape*. Edmonton, Alberta: Athabasca University Press.

Johnston, Barbara Rose, and Holly M. Barker. 2008. *Consequential Damages of Nuclear War: The Rongelap Report*. Walnut Creek, CA: Left Coast Press.

Jorgensen, Dan. 2014. "Mining Narratives and Multiple Geographies in Papua New Guinea: Ok Tedi, the Emerald Cave and Lost Tribes." *Journal de la Société des Océanistes* 138–139(1): 23–36

———. 2016. "The Garden and Beyond: The Dry Season, the Ok Tedi Shutdown, and the Footprint of the 2015 El Niño Drought." *Oceania* 86(1): 25–39.

Keen, David. 1994. *The Benefits of Famine: A Political Economy of Famine and Relief in Southwestern Sudan, 1983–1989*. Princeton, NJ: Princeton University Press.

Kelly, John E. 2008. "Contemplating Cahokia's Collapse." In *Global Perspectives on the Collapse of Complex Systems*, ed. J. A. Railey and R. M. Reycraft, pp.147–168. Albuquerque, NM: Maxwell Museum of Anthropology. Anthropological Papers No. 8.

Kim, Eleana. 2014. "The Flight of Cranes: Militarized Nature at the North Korea-South Korea Border." *Asian Environments: Connections across Borders, Landscapes, and Times*, Ursula Münster, et al., eds. RCC Perspectives, no. 3, pp. 65–70.

———. 2016. "Toward an Anthropology of Landmines: Rogue Infrastructure and Military Waste in the Korean DMZ." *Cultural Anthropology* 31(2): 162–187.

Kirsch, Stuart. 2006. *Reverse Anthropology: Indigenous Analysis of Social and Environmental Relations in New Guinea*. Stanford, CA: Stanford University Press.

———. 2014. *Mining Capitalism: The Relationship between Corporations and Their Critics*. Oakland: University of California Press.

Kufer, J., N. Grube, and M. Heinrich. 2006. "Cacao in Eastern Guatemala—A Sacred Tree with Ecological Significance." *Environment, Development and Sustainability* 8(4): 597–608.

Lahsen, Myanna. 2016. "Digging Deeper into the Why: Cultural Dimensions of Climate Change Skepticism Among Scientists." In *Climate Cultures: Anthropological Perspectives on Climate Change*, ed. Jessica Barnes and M. R. Dove, pp. 221–248. New Haven, CT: Yale University Press.

Lambert, Patricia M. 2013. "Violent Injury and Death in a Prehistoric Farming Community of Southwestern Colorado: The Osteological Evidence from Sleeping Ute Mountain." In *The Routledge Handbook of the Bioarchaeology of Human Conflict,* ed. Christopher Knüsel and Martin Smith, pp. 308–332. Abingdon, UK: Routledge.

Lansing, John Stephen. 2006. *Perfect Order: Recognizing Complexity in Bali*. Princeton, NJ: Princeton University Press.

Lansing, J. Stephen, and Thérèse A. de Vet. 2012. "The Functional Role of Balinese Water Temples: A Response to Critics." *Human Ecology* 40(3): 453–467.

Lansing, J. Stephen, John Schoenfelder, and Vernon Scarborough. 2006. "Rappaport's Rose: Structure, Agency, and Historical Contingency in Ecological Anthropology." In *Reimagining Political Ecology*, ed. A. Biersack and J. B. Greenberg, pp. 325–357. Durham, NC: Duke University Press.

Lee, Charles. 2002. "Environmental Justice: Building a Unified Vision of Health and the Environment." *Environmental Health Perspectives Supplements* 110: 141–144.

Leslie, Paul, and J. Terrence McCabe. 2013. "Response Diversity and Resilience in Social-Ecological Systems." *Current Anthropology* 54(2): 114–143.

Li, Tania Murray. 2014. *Land's End: Capitalist Relations on an Indigenous Frontier.* Durham, NC: Duke University Press.

Liebow, Edward. 2007. "Hanford, Tribal Risks, and Public Health in an Era of Forced Federalism." In *Half-Lives & Half-Truths: Confronting the Radioactive Legacies of the Cold War,* ed. B. R. Johnston, pp. 145–163. Santa Fe, NM: School for Advanced Research Press.

Lu, Flora. 2010. "Patterns of Indigenous Resilience in the Amazon: A Case Study of Huaorani Hunting in Ecuador." *Journal of Ecological Anthropology* 14(1): 5–21.

MacCormack, Carol P., and Marilyn Strathern. 1980. *Nature, Culture, and Gender.* New York: Cambridge University Press.

Macdonald, Fraser. 2017. "Cosmology and Crisis in Oksapmin, Papua New Guinea." *Oceania* 156–172.

Maffi, Luisa. 2005. "Linguistic, Cultural, and Biological Diversity." *Annual Review of Anthropology* 34(1): 599–617.

Martin, Paul S., and Richard G. Klein. 1984. *Quaternary Extinctions: A Prehistoric Revolution.* Tucson: University of Arizona Press.

Masquelier, Adeline. 2006. "Why Katrina's Victims Aren't Refugees: Musings on a 'Dirty' Word." *American Anthropologist* 108(4): 735–743.

McCaffrey, Katherine T. 2009. "Environmental Struggle After the Cold War: New Forms of Resistance to the U. S. Military in Vieques, Puerto Rico." In *Bases of Empire: The Global Struggle against U. S. Military Posts,* ed. Catherine Lutz, pp. 218–242. New York: New York University Press.

McCay, Bonnie J., and James M. Acheson. 1987. *The Question of the Commons: The Culture and Ecology of Communal Resources.* Tucson: University of Arizona Press.

McElroy, Ann. 2008. *Nunavut Generations: Change and Continuity in Canadian Inuit Communities.* Long Grove, IL: Waveland Press.

———. 2013. "Sedna's Children: Climate Change and Food Security." In *Environmental Anthropology: Future Directions,* ed. H. Kopnina and E. Shoreman-Ouimet, pp. 205–222. New York: Routledge.

McElroy, Ann, and Patricia K. Townsend. 2015. *Medical Anthropology in Ecological Perspective.* 6th ed. Boulder, CO: Westview Press.

McElwee, Pamela D. 2016. *Forests Are Gold: Trees, People, and Environmental Rule in Vietnam.* Seattle: University of Washington Press.

McGuire, Thomas R. 1997. "The Last Northern Cod." *Journal of Political Ecology* 4: 41–54.

Miller, Daniel. 2008. *The Comfort of Things.* Cambridge, UK: Polity Press.

Milton, Kay. 1996. *Environmentalism and Cultural Theory: Exploring the Role of Anthropology in Environmental Discourse.* London; New York: Routledge.

———. 2002. *Loving Nature: Towards an Ecology of Emotion.* London: Routledge.

Moore-Nall, Anita. 2015. "The Legacy of Uranium Development on or Near Indian Reservations and Health Implications Rekindling Public Awareness." *Geosciences.* 5(1):15–29.

Moran, Emilio F. 1993. *Through Amazonian Eyes: The Human Ecology of Amazonian Populations.* Iowa City: University of Iowa Press.

———. 2008. *Human Adaptability: An Introduction to Ecological Anthropology.* 3rd ed. Boulder, CO: Westview Press.

Nazarea, Virginia D. 1998. *Cultural Memory and Biodiversity.* Tucson: University of Arizona Press.

Netting, Robert McC. 1981. *Balancing on an Alp: Ecological Change and Continuity in a Swiss Mountain Community.* Cambridge: Cambridge University Press.

———. 1986. *Cultural Ecology.* 2nd ed. Long Grove, IL: Waveland Press.

Ngade, Ivo, et al. 2016. "Washing Away Ebola: Environmental Stress, Rumor, and Ethnomedical Response in a Deadly Epidemic." In *A Companion to the Anthropology of Environmental Health,* ed. Merrill Singer, pp. 157–172. New York: John Wiley & Sons.

Nichols, Theresa, Fikret Berkes, Norman B. Snow, and Dyanna Jolly. 2004. "Climate Change and Sea Ice: Local Observations from the Canadian Western Arctic." *Arctic* 57(1): 68–79.

Nichter, Mark. 1987. "Kyasanur Forest Disease: An Ethnography of a Disease of Development." *Medical Anthropology Quarterly* 1: 406–423.

Ok Tedi Mining, Ltd. 2017. *2016 Historical Statistics.* http://www.oktedi.com/media-items/reports/corporate/historical-statistics

Oliver-Smith, Anthony. 2013. "Disaster Risk Reduction and Climate Change Adaptation: The View from Applied Anthropology." *Human Organization* 72(4): 275–282.

O'Reilly, Jessica. 2016. "Sensing the Ice: Field science, Models, and Expert Intimacy with Knowledge." *Journal of the Royal Anthropological Institute* 22(S1): 27–45.

———. 2017. *The Technocratic Antarctic: An Ethnography of Scientific Expertise and Environmental Governance.* Ithaca, NY: Cornell University Press.

Orlove, Benjamin S., John C. H. Chiang, and Mark A. Cane. 2000. "Forecasting Andean Rainfall and Crop Yield from the Influence of El Niño on Pleiades Visibility." *Nature* 403(6765): 68–71.

Paulson, Susan, and Lisa L. Gezon, eds. 2005. *Political Ecology Across Spaces, Scales, and Social Groups.* New Brunswick, NJ: Rutgers University Press.

Pew Research Center. 2017. "The Changing Global Religious Landscape." Pewresearch.org/fact-tank. Accessed August 24, 2017.

Plumptre, Andrew J. et al. 2016. "Catastrophic Decline of World's Largest Primate: 80% Loss of Grauer's Gorilla (*Gorilla beringei graueri*) Population Justifies Critically Endangered Status." *PLoS ONE* 11(10): e0162697.

Posey, Darrell Addison, and Graham Dutfield. 1996. *Beyond Intellectual Property: Toward Traditional Resource Rights for Indigenous Peoples and Local Communities.* Ottawa: International Development Research Centre.

Puri, Rajindra K. 2005. *Deadly Dances in the Bornean Rainforest: Hunting Knowledge of the Penan Benalui.* Leiden: KITLV.

Rappaport, Roy A. 1968. *Pigs for the Ancestors: Ritual in the Ecology of a New Guinea People.* New Haven, CT: Yale University Press.

———. 1984. *Pigs for the Ancestors: Ritual in the Ecology of a New Guinea People.* 2nd ed. New Haven, CT: Yale University Press., (Reissued Long Grove, IL: Waveland Press, 2000.)

———. 1999. *Ritual and Religion in the Making of Humanity.* Cambridge, UK: Cambridge University Press.

Rasmussen, Mattias Borg. 2015. *Andean Waterways: Resource Politics in Highland Peru.* Seattle: University of Washington Press.

Rathje, William L., and Cullen Murphy. 1992. *Rubbish!: The Archaeology of Garbage.* New York: HarperCollins.

Read, Daniel J. 2016. "Legitimacy, Access, and the Gridlock of Tiger Conservation: Lessons from Melghat and the History of Central India." *Regional Environmental Change* 16(Supplement 1): S141–S151.

Robbins, Paul, and Julie Sharp. 2003. "The Lawn-Chemical Economy and Its Discontents." *Antipode* 35(5): 955–979.

Roosevelt, Anna. 1989. "Resource Management in Amazonia before the Conquest: Beyond Ethnographic Projection." *Advances in Economic Botany* 7: 30–62.

Rose, Deborah, Diana James, and Christine Watson. 2003. *Indigenous Kinship with the Natural World in New South Wales.* Hurstville, NSW, Australia: NSW National Parks and Wildlife Service.

Ross, Eric Barry. 1978. "Food Taboos, Diet, and Hunting Strategy: The Adaptation to Animals in Amazon Cultural Ecology." *Current Anthropology* 19(1): 1–36.

Ruddle, Kenneth et al. 1978. *Palm Sago: A Tropical Starch from Marginal Lands.* Honolulu: Published for the East-West Center by the University Press of Hawaii.

Sahlins, Marshall David, Elman Rogers Service, and Thomas G. Harding. 1960. *Evolution and Culture.* Ann Arbor: University of Michigan Press.

Sandom, Christopher et al. 2014. "Global late Quaternary Megafauna Extinctions Linked to Humans, not Climate Change." *Proceedings of the Royal Society B* 281: 20133254. doi: 10.1098/rspb.2013.3254 Available at: http://rspb.royalsocietypublishing.org/content/royprsb/281/1787/20133254.full.pdf

Schuetze, Christy. 2015. "Narrative Fortresses: Crisis Narratives and Conflict in the Conservation of Mount Gorongosa, Mozambique." *Conservation and Society* 13(2): 142–153.

Seton, Kathryn A., and John J. Bradley. 2004. "'When You Have No Law You Are Nothing': Cane Toads, Social Consequences and Management Issues." *Asia Pacific Journal of Anthropology* 5(3): 205–225.

Shepard, Glenn H., et al. 2012. "Hunting in Ancient and Modern Amazonia: Rethinking Sustainability." *American Anthropologist* 114(4): 652–667.

Sillitoe, Paul. 2006. "Ethnobiology and Applied Anthropology: Rapprochement of the Academic with the Practical." *Journal of the Royal Anthropological Institute* 12(Suppl. 1): 119–142.

Simons, Gary F., and Charles D. Fennig (eds.). 2017. *Ethnologue: Languages of the World, Twentieth edition.* Dallas, Texas: SIL International. Available at: http://www.ethnologue.com

Singer, Merrill. 2009. *Introduction to Syndemics: A Critical Systems Approach to Public and Community Health.* San Francisco, CA: Jossey-Bass/John Wiley & Sons.

Slater, David H. and Rika Morioka. 2014. "Micro-politics of Radiation: Young Mothers Looking for a Voice in Post-3.11 Fukushima." *Critical Asian Studies* 46(3): 485–508.

Spears, Ellen Griffith. 2014. *Baptized in PCBs: Race, Pollution, and Justice in an All-American Town.* Chapel Hill: University of North Carolina Press.

Sponsel, Leslie E. 2012. *Spiritual Ecology: A Quiet Revolution*. Santa Barbara, CA: Praeger/ABC-CLIO, LLC.

Sponsel, Leslie, and Poranee Natadecha-Sponsel. 2003. "Buddhist Views of Nature and the Environment." In *Nature Across Cultures*, ed. H. Selin and A. Kalland, pp. 351–392. Boston, MA: Kluwer.

Stawkowski, Magdalena E. 2016. "'I am a radioactive mutant': Emergent Biological Subjectivities at Kazakstan's Semipalatinsk Nuclear Test Site." *American Ethnologist* 43(1): 144–157.

Steward, Julian Haynes. 1955. *Theory of Culture Change: The Methodology of Multilinear Evolution*. Urbana: University of Illinois Press.

Stoffle, Richard W., and Richard Arnold. 2003. "Confronting the Angry Rock: American Indians' Situated Risks from Radioactivity." *Ethnos: Journal of Anthropology* 68(2): 230–248.

Stone, Glenn Davis. 2010. *The Anthropology of Genetically Modified Crops*. Annual Review of Anthropology 39: 381–400.

Stonich, Susan C. 1993. *"I Am Destroying the Land!": The Political Ecology of Poverty and Environmental Destruction in Honduras*. Boulder, CO: Westview Press.

Storey, Rebecca. 1992. "Children of Copán: Issues in Paleopathology and Paleodemography." *Ancient Mesoamerica* 3(1): 161–167.

Thomas, R. Brooke. 1976. "Energy Flow at High Altitude." In *Man in the Andes: Multidisciplinary Study of High-altitude Quechua*, ed. P. T. Baker and M. A. Little, pp. 379–404. Stroudsburg, PA: Dowden Hutchinson & Ross.

———. 1997. "Wandering toward the Edge of Adaptability: Adjustments of Andean People to Change." In *Human Adaptability Past, Present, and Future: The First Parkes Foundation Workshop, Oxford, January 1994*, ed. S. J. Ulijaszek and R. Huss-Ashmore, pp. 183–232. New York: Oxford University Press.

Tilt, Bryan. 2006. "Perceptions of Risk from Industrial Pollution in China: A Comparison of Occupational Groups." *Human Organization* 65(2): 115–127.

Townsend, Patricia. 1974. "Sago Production in a New Guinea Economy." *Human Ecology* 2(3): 217–236.

Townsend, Patricia, and William Townsend. 2003. "Assessing an Assessment: The Ok Tedi Mine." http://www.millenniumassessment.org/documents/bridging/papers/townsend.patricia.pdf

———. 2018. "On the Fringe: First Fieldwork in the Upper Sepik, 1966–67." In *First Fieldwork: Pacific Anthropology, 1960–1985*, ed. Laura Tamakoshi. Honolulu: University of Hawaii Press.

Townsend, William H. 1969. "Stone and Steel Tool Use in a New Guinea Society." *Ethnology* 8(2): 199–205.

UNEP (United National Environmental Program). 1999. *Cultural and Spiritual Values of Biodiversity*. London: Intermediate Technology Publications for the United Nations Environment Programme.

USEPA (United States Environmental Protection Agency). 2016. Climate Change Indicators: Health and Society. https://www.epa.gov/climate-indicators/health-society

Vayda, Andrew P. 1999. *Finding Causes of the 1997–98 Indonesian Forest Fires: Problems and Possibilities*. Jakarta: World Wide Fund for Nature—Indonesia.

Vine, David. 2009. *Island of Shame: The Secret History of the U. S. Military Base on Diego Garcia*. Princeton: Princeton University Press.

———. 2015. *Base Nation: How U. S. Military Bases Abroad Harm America and the World*. New York: Metropolitan Books, Henry Holt and Company.

Wackernagel, Mathis, and William E. Rees. 1996. *Our Ecological Footprint: Reducing Human Impact on the Earth*. Gabriola Island, BC: New Society Publishers.

Walker, Michael Madison. 2015. "Producing Gorongosa: Space and the Environmental Politics of Degradation in Mozambique." *Conservation and Society* 13(2): 129–140.

Walsh, Vivien, and Jordan Goodman. 2002. "From Taxol to Taxol®: The Changing Identities and Ownership of an Anti-Cancer Drug." *Medical Anthropology* 21(3/4): 307–336.

Webster, David L. 2002. *The Fall of the Ancient Maya: Solving the Mystery of the Maya Collapse*. New York: Thames & Hudson.

Webster, David, AnnCorinne Freter, and Nancy Gonlin. 2000. *Copán: The Rise and Fall of an Ancient Maya Kingdom*. Fort Worth, TX: Harcourt.

Wenzel, George W. 1991. *Animal Rights, Human Rights: Ecology, Economy, and Ideology in the Canadian Arctic*. Toronto: University of Toronto Press.

West, Paige. 2006. *Conservation Is Our Government Now: The Politics of Ecology in Papua New Guinea*. Durham, NC: Duke University Press.

———. 2016. *Dispossession and the Environment: Rhetoric and Inequality in Papua New Guinea*. New York: Columbia University Press.

West, Paige, James Igoe, and Dan Brockington. 2006. "Parks and Peoples: The Social Impact of Protected Areas." *Annual Review of Anthropology* 35: 251–277.

White, Leslie A. 1959. *The Evolution of Culture: The Development of Civilization to the Fall of Rome*. New York: McGraw-Hill.

Wilk, Richard. 2002. "Consumption, Human Needs, and Global Environmental Change." *Global Environmental Change* 12: 5–13.

Wilson, E. O. 2016. *Half-Earth: Our Planet's Fight for Life*. New York: Liveright Publishing, a division of W.W. Norton.

Winterhalder, Bruce. 2001. "The Behavioural Ecology of Hunter Gatherers." In *Hunter-gatherers: An Interdisciplinary Perspective*, ed. C. Panter-Brick, R. Layton and P. Rowley-Conwy, pp. 12–38. New York: Cambridge University Press.

Wolf, Eric. 1972. "Ownership and Political Ecology." *Anthropological Quarterly* 45: 201–205.

Index